GARLAND STUDIES IN

THE HISTORY OF AMERICAN LABOR

T0347638

edited by

STUART BRUCHEY
ALLAN NEVINS PROFESSOR EMERITUS
COLUMBIA UNIVERSITY

FEMALE CORPORATE CULTURE AND CULTURE AND THE NEW SOUTH

WOMEN IN BUSINESS BETWEEN THE WORLD WARS

MAUREEN CARROLL GILLIGAN

Routledge
Taylor & Francis Group

LONDON AND NEW YORK

First published 1999 by Garland publishing, Inc.

Published 2018 by Routledge
2 Park Square, Milton Park, Abingdon, Oxon OX14 4RN
52 Vanderbilt Avenue, New York, NY 10017

First issued in paperback 2018

Routledge is an imprint of the Taylor & Francis Group, an informa business

Library of Congress Cataloging-in-Publication Data

Gilligan, Maureen Carroll, 1961–
    Female corporate culture and the new South : women in
business between the world wars / Maureen Carroll Gilliogan.
        p.   cm. — (Garland studies in the history of American
labor)
    Includes bibliographical references and index.
    ISBN 0-8153-3184-3 (alk. paper)
    1. Women—Employment—United States—History—20th
century. 2. Women clerks—United States—History—20th century. 3. Sex role in the work environment—United States—
History—20th century. 4. Working class women—United States—
History—20th century. I. Title. II. Series.
HD6095.G49 1999
331.4'0975—dc21

                                        99-19280

            ISBN 13: 978-1-138-86387-3 (pbk)
            ISBN 13: 978-0-8153-3184-1 (hbk)

Contents

Tables

TABLES

Introduction

Seventeen-year-old Stella Brady came to Atlanta from Concord, Georgia in 1924 to look for clerical work. Despite arriving there without completing high school, she was optimistic that she could find employment. Other girls from Concord and agricultural towns like it had found work as typists, stenographers, and clerks. She could too. Desperation had forced Stella to leave her home and travel the forty miles to Atlanta. Her father died when she was thirteen leaving her mother with five young children to raise. Stella was the eldest. Thus, at seventeen, she left home feeling duty-bound to contribute to her family's welfare. Upon entering an Atlanta business school, Stella realized her aptitude for clerical work fell considerably below her ambition. "I didn't do very good; I was homesick" she recalled, "I was so young and so, well, just didn't know the city." She returned to Concord to keep books for her uncle, "recording the cotton futures and making change for the big store. I did whatever he asked me to do." In January 1925, she returned to Atlanta again seeking work. She filled several more clerical jobs before she married in 1927. Although wed, Stella continued to work and attend business courses to sharpen her typing and shorthand skills. In March 1934, she pursued what appeared to be a temporary position with the Georgia Parent Teacher Association. She stayed for fifty-one years.[1]

Between 1924 and 1934, Stella had prepared herself for a clerical position that would support her through the Depression, widowhood, and World War II. Although living in Atlanta, she continued to provide for her family in Concord. Later, after her husband died, she secured a home and lived independently without the security of an extended family and marriage.

Stella Brady's story is only one example that illustrates how important clerical work opportunities were for southern women during the 1920s and the 1930s. Atlanta offices employed thousands of Stella Bradys, and this work experience shaped a generation of women living between the wars. This multitude of female office workers gained financial and social independence unparalleled by any other generation of educated women except, perhaps, teachers and the elite. In the South, clerical occupations engaged a class of white females that had rarely or never entered public work places before. In the post-World War I years, this female workforce clearly played a significant role in the process of urbanization. As Atlanta's economy and physical development expanded, and the city adopted a corporate philosophy and identity, female office workers became symbols of opportunity and modernization. These women workers more than symbolized the modern woman; they helped transform the role working woman had in civic identity.

Office work greatly altered working women's relationships with their families and in their communities. Municipal educational programs changed to suit the needs of the business community and trained women to enter corporations, in their proper place. As more women entered offices, these work places reorganized to accommodate new work methods and new gender relationships. Women's participation in the white-collar workforce greatly altered their relationships within families and introduced the unique dilemma of working middle-class wives. Corporate and community reactions to these changes in women's workforce participation proved imaginative, sometimes supportive, but almost always inspired and limited by socially sanctioned gender roles and expectations. Women's office work during the 1920s cracked open the door to revolutionary change in community gender roles. The Depression halted most of the strides made by women and placed them in vulnerable positions again.

Throughout the United States, office work opened avenues of opportunity for social and familial independence, varied work, travel, economic stability, and the possibility of a life-long career for women that paralleled men's professional lives. This study examines the Atlanta female office worker within her work environment, as a citizen, and in her social activities. In each of these areas, women encountered challenges that required them to examine existing gender roles and redefine or adapt these roles to meet social change brought on by urbanization and corporate capitalism. Through these processes, the dilution of regional distinctiveness is also evident, which brought southern female clerical workers closer to national models.

The study is organized thematically rather than chronologically. Change occurred over time, but within the period 1919-1940, the cultural changes held more drama than the passage of time. The transformation of a small, predominantly male clerical workforce into a large occupational group with significant female participation had occurred by the end of World War I. Many sources helped characterize the post-war female clerical workforce. Government labor and population census studies defined the demographic makeup of Atlanta's female clerical workforce. Atlanta business histories and scholarly discussions of corporate capitalism and culture provided context for women's role in urbanization and occupational change. Women's organizational records helped illustrate gender roles in both the occupational and civic arenas. Oral history interviews served as supplemental sources to the documentary data and personalized the discussions of work roles, employee and employer relationships. In their own words, women discuss their workplaces, their family and community ties, and the urban environment.

Chapter One describes women's introduction into offices and summarizes the major themes of clerical labor history. This chapter also introduces the reader to scholarly clerical work histories and outlines the growth of the Atlanta female workforce within the region and the United States.

Chapter Two focuses on women's office work through the eyes of management and the corporation. In 1931, the Women's Bureau of the U.S. Department of Labor conducted surveys in seven American cities among women in clerical positions.[2] Published as Women's Bureau Bulletin Number 120, the survey addressed the concerns of working women outside of the industrial sector and in areas of the country, including the South, which had been neglected by previous surveys of working women in established "female occupations."

Ethel Erickson of the Women's Bureau collected data in Atlanta between April and June of 1931, from fifty-seven offices employing white women and two employing black women. It included over 3,700 women, approximately 40 percent of the city's total female clerical workforce. Besides examining the physical characteristics of the 1930 workforce, the survey illustrates management practices among many prominent Atlanta firms and the concerns of the Women's Bureau. Although the survey focused on quantifiable labor issues including wages, education, and opportunity for advancement, it hints at subtler management practices that equally affected female clerical labor, particularly the persistence of paternalism in office environments.

Chapter Three is a case study of an Atlanta firm, Retail Credit Company, that employed a large female clerical workforce. Through a combined system of paternalism and rationalized labor management, southern corporations created a milieu wherein women performed most of the menial office work, but they rarely questioned company tactics or their inability to achieve significant business success.

Denied access to positions of power or achievement within the firm, some southern working women turned toward civicism. The term civicism characterizes a personal identification with civic activities and urban growth. Atlanta's business community expected the elite, and to some extent its working population, to support vigorous city building through morally inspired secular activities, including commercial pursuits. Chapter Four examines the culture of civic boosterism in Atlanta, and how the male business elite influenced white-collar women through education programs and control of women's social welfare activities. The business culture maintained a powerful influence on all civic activities in Atlanta and directly affected women's office work by promoting occupational training in the public schools and advancing the edifying aspects of female office work. Several women's service organizations, such as the Young Women's Christian Association (YWCA) and the Women's Division of the Chamber of Commerce, catered their agendas to the business community, while they hoped to serve the needs of the working woman.

By contrast, Chapter Five illustrates the emergence of business women's organizations and a distinctive form of female civicism. Three organizations, the Atlanta Chapter of the Business and Professional Women's Clubs (BPWC), the Atlanta Young Women's Christian Association, and the Women's Division of the Atlanta Chamber of Commerce, represented and served distinct economic and social interests among business women in Atlanta. They illustrate the nature of business women's civicism and how their activities contributed to the civic ideal.

Chapter Six examines the effects of the Depression years on gains made by Atlanta clerical workers, club women, and working women in general. The Federal Emergency Relief Administration (FERA) in Georgia was federalized early in the program. FERA chief Harry Hopkins appointed a woman, Gay B. Shepperson, to administer federal funds in the state. Based in Atlanta, and aided by skilled and capable female administrators, Shepperson created viable women's emergency relief programs for skilled and unskilled Georgia women and employed hundreds of out-of-work female clerical workers. Atlanta and the metropolitan counties of Fulton and Dekalb received the bulk of clerical labor assistance, particularly in the organization of municipal and county records.

One of the appealing aspects of clerical work lie in its relative stability as an occupational choice. Although employers reduced their workforces throughout the Depression years, clerical workers suffered lower unemployment rates than other groups of female workers. The 1932 Women's Bureau survey illustrated minor economic impacts upon clerical workforces. Commonly, clerical workers suffered because pay increases diminished or disappeared, and employers increased work loads, or reduced benefits and vacations. Despite these losses, women kept their jobs and accepted the reductions as short term hardships.

The losses for business women throughout the Depression were psychological as well as economic. Women repeatedly voiced feelings of insecurity and fear of the future stemming from their inadequate salaries or limited opportunities. In Atlanta, women workers expressed uneasiness about the precarious nature of their employment. Popular newspaper columnist, Mildred Seydell of the *Georgian*, received numerous letters from women during the Depression years. Women also wrote to the Federal Emergency Relief Administration in Georgia and Washington D.C., asking for assistance and illustrating well the condition of the entire nation.

The following chapters describe the work relationships and the secular organizations that emerged as a result of women's participation in clerical occupations. Regional distinctiveness is present in the interstices where individuals and corporations did not meet and needed a bridge, or where women's defined social roles, in the home or in their social organizations, linked these job-related identities with custom or gender boundaries that they could expand to meet their changing role in cities.

NOTES

1. Mrs. Stella Brady, interview by author, Tape recording, Atlanta, Georgia, 21 April 1987.

2. Ethel Erickson, "The Employment of Women in Offices" Bulletin No. 120, Women's Bureau (Washington: GPO, 1934):

Female Corporate Culture
and the New South

CHAPTER 1

Urbanization, Clerical Work, and the Modern Southern Woman

By the end of World War I, the United States was recognized worldwide as an industrialized and urbanized nation. Factories that had produced a growing body of consumer products such as household goods, ready-to-wear clothing, and food products in the 1910s converted to war materiel production in 1917 and 1918. Technological breakthroughs in agricultural production greatly enhanced the United State's ability to feed the warring armies of Great Britain and France. By the war's end, conversion of wartime industrial and agricultural production to domestic goods and services greatly altered women's pre-war work roles and opportunities. Women participated in this transformation through their work, their roles in families, and the civic networks established by and for women. The nation's female nonagricultural labor force grew steadily throughout the period 1880 to 1930, and female clerical labor force participation accounted for much of this growth. The war greatly accelerated the pace of women's office work participation, which increased nearly 50 percent from the pre-war decade.[1] In Atlanta, white women increased their public labor force participation from 16 percent in 1890 to 28.9 percent in 1930 (See Table 1.1). Atlanta's female labor force in 1890 was one of the smallest in the nation, but was comparable to other southern cities, such as Charleston, Nashville, New Orleans, and Richmond. By 1930, Atlanta's white female labor force participation more closely matched the rates recorded in some of the nation's well-established cities than it did the female workforce participation in southern urban centers. Also by 1930, the city's clerical workforce participation had leapt ahead of the national urban average, which hovered at 30 percent.

Table 1.1: White Female Labor Force Participation & Proportion of Employed Clerical Workers, 1890 & 1930, Selected Cities

City	1890		1930	
	Labor Force Participation	Clerical	Labor Force Participation	Clerical
Atlanta	16.2	5.4	28.9	40.6
Boston	30.0	5.6	32.1	27.8
Charleston	16.2	2.3		
Columbus	16.5	5.0	27.1	27.8
Nashville	15.9	4.1	25.6	32.8
Oakland			25.2	29.2
New Orleans	17.7	1.9	23.8	28.6
Richmond	17.5	4.1	29.1	33.9

Source: Elyce Rotella, *From Home to Office*, Appendix B, "The Urban Sample".

Between the 1880s and the 1920s, women entered offices and contributed to the rapid growth of white collar workforces that cities like Atlanta grew upon, thus playing a significant role in the process of urbanization through their workforce participation.[2] Throughout the 1920s and 1930s, the wages, working conditions, and availability of office work surpassed industrial work opportunities and made clerical work an appealing occupation for Atlanta women.[3] Trade and clerical occupations employed approximately 25 percent of the 1920 female working population. Clerical employment alone engaged approximately 19 percent of the 1920 Atlanta female working population over the age of ten. Manufacturing and mechanical industries employed approximately 15 percent of Atlanta's working females.[4] By the end of the decade, Atlanta's female clerical workforce had increased by a third. Only domestic and personal service, which engaged approximately 50 percent of the total female workforce, employed more women than clerical occupations, and these servants and laundresses were predominantly black (See Table 1.2, "Atlanta Female Workforce Participation, Selected Occupations, 1910-1940".) The regional racial phenomena that bifurcated Atlanta's female working population literally created two groups of Atlanta working women, one symbolized by the typewriter, the other by the mop.[5] The image of the early female clerical worker, reflected in national and Atlanta newspapers, magazines, business periodicals, popular literature, and among women's organizations, identified them as a single occupational group. The nearly all-white, youthful clerical workforce inspired this literature. Except for a few black-owned establishments, which employed black women for office work, the clerical workforce in Atlanta was white with a median age of twenty-five.[6]

Race often has defined the difference between national and southern economic growth and cultural trends, and has helped create a historical genre defined as southern distinctiveness. In clerical work occupations, racial segregation followed the regional trend mirrored in social settings. Black women did not have the opportunity to enter clerical work as easily as white women did. No public school office training programs existed for black students, and few employers beckoned even the overqualified black college graduates seeking clerical work. The gender isolation and hierarchy of clerical work exhibited in southern offices may better define regional or southern distinctiveness than race. Although gender segregation was endemic to office occupations, certain cultural beliefs and practices in the South likely contributed to the persistence of employment practices that decreased women's ability to rise occupationally in southern offices. These southern peculiarities are explored throughout this study.

Although Atlanta's female clerical workforce growth paralleled the nation's on many levels, it is unique because southern urban expansion accompanied the increase of commercial professions, especially in the twentieth century. Established as a post-Civil War transportation and mercantile center, Atlanta entered the twentieth century poised to dominate the region as a versatile financial, service, and manufacturing metropolis. The rapid expansion of real estate, banking, insurance, and transportation trade interests in the city prior to 1918, affected the urban fabric, its working population, and the identity of the city.

By 1920, cities throughout the U.S. employed between 11 and 17 percent of their workforces in clerical occupations, and approximately 50 percent of that workforce was female.[7] Atlanta's clerical workforce participation in 1920 (14 percent) compared more favorably to northeastern cities with larger populations, including Boston and Pittsburgh or to emerging regional centers exhibiting similar economic and occupational growth patterns such as Denver, Houston, and San

Table 1.2: Atlanta Female Workforce Participation Selected Occupations, 1910-1940

Occupations	1910		1920		1930		1940	
Female population	25,712		32,250		47,124		48923	
	Number	Percent	Number	Percent	Number	Percent	Number	Percent
Dressmakers & Seamstresses (nonfactory)	1395	5.4	908	2.8	825	1.7	731	1.5
Milliners & Millinery Dealers	380	1.4	275	—	279	—	NL	
Clothing industries (factory)	174	—	821	2.5	1230	2.6	1328	3
Food industries	155	—	482	1.5	382	—	482	9.8
Printing & publishing (factory)	158	—	147	—	199	—	NL	
Textile operatives	709	2.7	643*	1.9	728*	1.5	1056	2.1
Sewers & machine operators (factory	586	2.2	NL	—	NL	—	NL	
Telephone operators	288	1.1	683	2.1	923	1.9	749	1.5
Clerks in stores	190	—	234	—	236	—	NL	
Saleswomen in stores	740	2.8	1315	4	2061	4.3	2386	4.8

Table 1.2 (continued)

Occupations	1910 25,712 Number	1910 Percent	1920 32,250 Number	1920 Percent	1930 47,124 Number	1930 Percent	1940 48,923 Number	1940 Percent
Female population								
Teachers	775	3	1036	3.2	1684	3.5	1788	3.7
Nurses	446	1.7	621	1.9	1112	2.3	1349	2.8
Clerical	2013	8.1	6112	18.9	9251	19.6	11,155	22.8
Retail Dealers	131	—	173	—	256	—	378	7.7
Boarding & Lodging House keepers	485	1.8	414	1.2	547	1.1	693	1.4
Barbers, Hairdressers & Manicurists	NL	—	434	1.3	475	1	842'd	1.7

Source: U.S. Department of Commerce, *Thirteenth Census*, 1910; *Fourteenth Census*, 1930; *Sixteenth Census*, 1940.

• In 1920, the census differentiated between cotton, silken, and woolen mills in the Atlanta area. The numbers represented in this table are cotton mill workers who occupied the most positions.

NL Not listed as an occupation.

— Less than one percent of the total female working population represented.

Francisco than to other southern cities. Although female participation rates are historically high in southern cities because of black female labor in domestic and personal service occupations, it does not diminish the contribution female clerical labor made to the growth of southern cities like Atlanta.

Atlanta's total workforce participation outstripped most of the region's cities, except New Orleans, although proportionally southern urban women's employment was similar in all cities. Atlanta women composed approximately 37 percent of the city's working population. Comparably, Richmond women composed 35 percent of its workforce; in Nashville and Memphis, women made up 34 percent of the employed population. Predominantly an industrial center, Birmingham had a smaller female working population (28 percent). Among these regional cities, the female workforce shared similar occupational distribution. Consistently, women composed three-fourths of the domestic and personal service workers in southern cities. Atlanta, Richmond, and Nashville shared sexually balanced clerical populations (averaging between 43 and 47 percent female). However, both Richmond and Nashville had more professional women than Atlanta did (See Table 1.3).

Atlanta's economy and workforce, exhibiting growth in the service and clerical sectors, typified the southern urban experience as the twentieth century unfolded. For southern women, these expanded areas provided occupational choices not available in the previous decades. Atlanta's diversified economy differed from the nation's largest urban centers, which had experienced urbanization through industrialization. As Atlanta's economy shifted from manufacturing and distribution of goods tied to its sizeable railroad development to finance and other service industries, the workforce and the urban fabric changed along with it. Female clerical workers played a significant role in these new urbanization trends, which were associated with the nonmanufacturing business community and symbolized by new skyscrapers and the movement of the central business district away from the railroad corridors.[8] Manufacturing still played an important role in Atlanta's economy prior to World War II, however, and city leaders strove to increase industrial capacity through the Forward Atlanta campaign in the mid-1920s. Despite these efforts, the city's image increasingly rested in figures like office products magnate Ivan Allen, banker Robert Maddox, and manufacturer and financier, Asa Candler, not industrial giants.

Table 1.3: Southern Region Female Workforces
Selected Occupations, 1920

City	Total	% Wm Employed	% Wm Clerical	Clerical	Domestic	Industrial	Professional
					% of Women in Selected Occupations		
Atlanta	98,952	33	20	43	75	17	40
Birmingham	79,152	25	16	38	77	6	39
Memphis	80,571	30	16	38	75	13	47
Nashville	55,254	32	18	47	76	18	47
Richmond	79,825	33	20	44	74	26	48
Houston	65,930	26	20	36	68	11	38

Source: U.S. Department of Commerce, *Fourteenth Census of the United States, 1920: Population*, I.

DEFINING WOMEN'S CLERICAL WORKFORCE HISTORY

Many scholars have studied the growth, feminization, proletarianization, and stabilization of the American female office workforce.[9] The transformation of middle-class clerical positions into the modern office hierarchy of low-level clerks and a chain of managers is treated thoroughly. These studies describe the antebellum male-dominated office, which consisted of a few autonomous clerks who were charged with a variety of duties including copying of documents, correspondence, and bookkeeping, and were nominally supervised by the proprietor or a senior clerk. The relationship between the clerk and his employer was familiar and often paternalistic. Within this relationship, class differences were obscured and often any shortcomings in the labor system were perceived as personal, rather than economic problems. However, the expansion of capitalist markets, the growth of transportation and communication systems, and technological innovations following the Civil War produced profound changes in the accounting of manufacturing, financial, and other business transactions. Thus, the scientific organization of offices and office work emerged. Informal or non-existent administrative hierarchies, common in small offices, failed to organize the detailed transactions of a burgeoning capitalist corporate economy. Small offices rarely employed the labor necessary to record these transactions, and large offices lacked systematic accounting and work organization. As a result, new organization techniques, which encompassed labor and task management emerged and often replaced the familiar relationship between the clerk and his employer.[10]

Women entered clerical occupations on the cusp of this change. The education level, availability, and volume of the female labor force complimented the needs of offices in flux and filled the gap between increased labor demands and streamlined procedures. Female clerical employment certainly contributed to the rapid and widespread adoption of modern office labor management. However, the introduction of women office workers did not create these changes. Both Cindy Aron and Margery Davies agree that American businesses forfeited personal paternalistic policies of management for more business-like ones, characterized by departmental division, administrative hierarchies, and specialized tasks, before feminization occurred. Efficiency and profit motives, not gender domination, motivated labor proletarianization.

Many women trained for and entered clerical jobs because they thought they were good jobs.

Aron and other scholars also emphasize that female clerical employment significantly altered business work environments by domesticating the office sphere, relaxing the decorous and often circumspect social relations between Victorian men and women, and creating precedents for female behavior within the office. Middle-class domestic female roles transferred well into late nineteenth-century offices, particularly the expression of familial obligations. Married and single women stressed their participation in family economies and how work in the public sphere expanded the definition of their domestic female roles. Once engaged in positions, employers often identified women as dependable and loyal workers, well suited for the low-level and segregated positions offered to them. Most women prepared for specific tasks within offices through business schools and were not expected to pursue independent or autonomous roles within the office. Male and female office workers assumed that domestic activities and emotional relationships within the family remained preeminent in women's lives. Whether married or single, work roles only added to these domestic responsibilities. The Victorian middle-class female model lasted well into the twentieth century and afforded a precedent for employers to enforce patriarchical values upon women's office work. Women office workers throughout the 1920s and 1930s often labored under rigid routines and mechanization for lower pay than their male counterparts and were also subject to paternalistic control over their behavior within and outside of the office.

Office work culture after World War I, while certainly less constrained by sexual uneasiness, remained influenced by the roles appropriated to women and by women, especially middle-class women, within the broader society. As women's office work participation expanded during the 1920s, it stimulated a gender-based consciousness among business women. The term "business woman," widely used by the 1920s, replaced the "office girl" nomenclature of the war years and placed these women in a distinctive laboring group composed of professionals and clerical workers. Throughout the United States, women employed in offices and the professions created clubs and associations that identified them principally as independent, career business women. Through these organizations, women created distinct civic roles for business women and promoted self-help among this laboring group. Neither middle-class reformers nor dilettante do-gooders, these working women strove to have their voices and their ideas distinguished from or at the very least heard among the consensus established by male urban civic pioneers.[11]

Many female office workers in Atlanta characterized themselves as members of distinct groups through their work roles, and political, religious, and social affiliations. Within office environments, or through clubs, neighborhoods, or churches Atlanta's business women found common ground, and these associations flesh out a portrait of the female clerical worker that is missing from discussions of feminization, rationalization, and class identity.

Although gender issues dominated discussions among critics and advocates of working women, economic necessity and the maintenance of established standards of living often compelled single and married women to work. The Women's Bureau of the Department of Labor, a strong supporter of women's right to work, focused its advocacy on disproving the pin money theory applied to female white-collar workers. This theory implied that middle-class women in offices worked primarily for luxuries for themselves or for their families. Increasingly during the 1920s and the 1930s, women's white-collar labor contributed to family economies. Historian Winifred Wandersee notes that "many American families owed their middle-class consumption patterns not to adequate wages for one person but to the presence of several wage earners in the family."[12]

Scholars attempting to define the class status of twentieth-century clerical workers explore the various types of white-collar employment and draw links between employment and class status. C. Wright Mills, describing white-collar occupations among females, included teachers, salespeople, and office workers. Mills attributes increased rationalization and the lowering of skill levels, universal high school education in large urban areas, and the growth of white-collar ranks to the decline in the status of white-collar work. In addition, Mills suggests that white collar's "claims for prestige are raised on the basis of consumption; but since consumption is limited by income, class position and status position intersect."[13] Ileen DeVault criticizes historical studies that limit discussions of class among clerical workers to white-collar occupational groups since these analyses do not address the majority of office workers who performed low-level clerical work. DeVault argues that evaluations of the class status of clerical workers should examine the changes in clerical workers' material condition, as well as occupational grouping, especially in the twentieth century. DeVault also notes that scholarly analyses of gender and feminization issues often fail to evaluate the economic conditions that impelled women to seek clerical work.[14] Harry Braverman concludes that the twentieth-century clerical worker's link to the nineteenth-century concept of middle-class office work was severed by the 1920s.[15]

Cindy Aron describes the clerical workers in federal offices in the mid-to-late nineteenth century as middle class. Federal clerical workers were the sons and daughters of proprietors and professionals, lived in middle-class residences, and partook in the social and financial amenities of middle-class life. These clerks owned their homes, educated their children, belonged to clubs and associations, and commonly engaged domestic servants. Although their social and economic connections separated these clerks from the skilled or manual laborer, their labor differed distinctly from traditional middle-class occupations of the period. Laboring for wages, middle-class clerks broke ranks with the entrepreneurs and professionals who defined the nineteenth-century American middle class. Several studies of clerical workers in England and in twentieth-century U.S. cities illustrate the dominant perception of clerical work as a middle-class occupation despite the economic reality.[16]

David Lockwood describes the deterioration of occupational opportunities among clerks in London in the late-nineteenth and early-twentieth century. Despite the loss of autonomy in the performance of their work, lower salaries, competition with foreign and female labor, and a decided change in the familiar relationship between the clerk and his employer, clerks in London counting houses clung to their identity as middle-class "gentlemen" clerks. "The world of the counting house," Lockwood notes, "formed an environment which, despite the objective, economic position of many clerical workers, was generally conducive to their estrangement from the mass of working men and to their identification with the entrepreneurial classes and [the] professional."[17] Gregory Anderson also illustrates the seductive pull of middle-class identity and paternalistic labor policies among clerks in Manchester and Liverpool in the late-nineteenth and early-twentieth centuries. Although the economic reality of clerical labor suggested a closer association with lower middle-class or working-class groups, English clerks maintained their badges of social respectability by channeling their earnings into club memberships, clothing, and private educations for their children. Altogether, the expansion of routine clerical positions at lowered salaries, increased office hierarchies and labor segmentation, and the disappearance of channels of upward mobility into the employer class, undermined the traditional paternal relationship clerks enjoyed with their employers but failed to convince them to create labor liaisons similar to other wage-earning groups. As a result, the National Union of Clerks accused the majority of clerks "of subscribing to a false class-consciousness which bore no relevance to economic realities."[18]

In the United States, Grace Hutchins, a Depression-era labor essayist, pointed to the increasing similarities between female clerical workers and industrial workers. She also roundly criticized groups like the Young Women's Christian Association (YWCA) for "cultivat[ing] notions of individual 'culture' as attainable by the woman worker who can raise herself above her fellows and become a success in the business or professional world."[19] She continues, "rare indeed is the bourgeois woman's club or organization that questions the profit system or the idea of individual advancement."[20] These criticisms pointedly blamed traditional middle-class female networks of ignoring the vast changes in female office work opportunities and limitations.

Although not as dogmatic as Hutchins, the Women's Bureau of the U.S. Department of Labor also recognized the growing likenesses among female wage-earning groups and turned its attention in the 1930s towards office workers. Spurred by the growth of the female clerical workforce, in 1932, Mary Anderson, the Director of the Women's Bureau of the U.S. Department of Labor, placed female clerical workers in the midst of industrial change. "The office worker has come to play an increasingly important role both in the production of goods and in the processes whereby production is linked with distribution."[21] Questions concerning the effects of mechanization and office organization motivated the Women's Bureau to undertake a series of studies of women in offices during 1931 and the early months of 1932. Preliminary data from these studies suggested that, although the clerical worker enjoyed better and more varied working conditions and some opportunities for advancement, the work performed in offices, "more and more approximate[s] factory work."[22] Clearly, by the 1930s, a shift in class status of the majority of office workers had occurred.

Despite the concerns of labor advocates, few women in 1920s offices recognized their class position—increasingly defined by their economic status—as tangential to working class or other laboring women. Clerical workers assumed that industrial or factory work carried lower social class connotations than similarly paid office work. Grace Coyle, a Secretary within the National YWCA wrote that "some working class women saw clerical work not only as more prestigious, but even as a means of rising out of the working class itself."[23]

Throughout the 1920s, feminists and women's organizations stressed the aesthetic importance of women's white-collar work, particularly self-fulfillment through professional careers. As Hutchins emphasized, contemporary feminists failed to recognize their class bias and that "the ideologies of feminism seldom reached working class women." Prevailing feminist thought affected few women outside of the professions, yet its ideological tenets were intended to address a common female white-collar audience. According to 1920s feminists, the benefits of female white-collar work lay in re-establishing productive roles for middle-class women lost in industrialization and urbanization. Women's passive roles as child nurturers and homemakers overshadowed the important economic roles women played in preindustrial or nonindustrial environments. Feminists believed that gainful employment, particularly in white-collar occupations, would elevate women's self-esteem, as well as their autonomy. The feminists' advocacy of self-fulfillment meshed well with the individualism ethos of the 1920s, especially among youthful workers.[24]

However, by the 1930s, threats to working women's positions subdued the feminists' rhetoric of individualism and self-fulfillment. A spate of restrictive federal and local legislation passed into law and diminished women's right to work, thus shifting the focus of feminist debates to justifications of why women worked and not why they should work. Increasingly, groups like the National Business and Professional Woman's Clubs, the Zonta Clubs, a professional women's organization, and the Women's Bureau found common ground urging economic reconstruction and advocating the supplementary role woman played in family economies. Lois Scharf laments that feminism in the 1930s suffered so harshly from the social and economic climate. "Issues seemingly unrelated to economic reconstruction were neglected," she notes, if not outrightly criticized by various working women's groups. The individualistic ideology of 1920s feminists fell prey to unemployment among women and severe criticism of working wives. The Depression economy intensified the competition for jobs and "reinforced the cultural assumptions concerning the proper sexual division of labor within family and society." Ironically, the middle-class audience courted by 1920s feminists adhered closely to traditional social roles and if possible did not utilize the labor of wives.[25] Winifred Wandersee suggests that for most women, outside work indicated women's commitment to family values as opposed to autonomy or independence. "Women had many unspoken personal reasons for engaging in work outside the home," she writes, "but during the 1930s, the overwhelming reason was still economic."[26]

Atlanta office workers belonged to class and occupational groups that had meaning based on what job they performed, what duties it entailed, and whom they worked for. Issues of feminism, class status, or labor segmentation resided in the periphery of women's day-to-day lives and may have been important to them but under different labels. What mattered to working women like Marie Cooper, who were educated, solidly middle class, and members of a small conservative urban community, was often reflected in family networks, work relationships, and secular and religious community involvement.

Marie Cooper worked as a private secretary for an Atlanta legal firm, formerly the legal counsel of the Coca-Cola Company. "My mother, myself, and my sister, she worked at Westminster College, she and her husband, the four of us moved to Atlanta," she recalled. "My older sister was already living here and married," she continued, "[and] then we bought this house, May 2, 1929." Marie never married and continued to support herself and contribute to the household on St. Charles Avenue. "During the war (World War II) [my sister] worked in the Bell Bomber plant. [My] brother-in-law worked. Mother had income on her own. We weren't penniless."[27]

Marie's life centered on her role as a provider, and it greatly affected her world view, especially her relationship to her family, her viability as a worker, and her role as a citizen within the Atlanta community. Marie's family played an essential role in her life and was the primary reason she worked. Outside of her family commitments, Marie placed greatest importance upon her membership to the Druid Hills Baptist Church and her involvement in domestic and foreign missionary activities. Marie identified the church as her link to the community. Many Atlanta working women, as members of prayer circles, filled social responsibilities and found spiritual satisfaction in their church work. Social identifications, and by inference class status, emerged and solidified in the secular and religious activities of Atlanta's citizens. Frequently, an individual's job and social activities delineated what social group she affiliated with, and these groups helped define the layers of an urban community. For Atlanta female clerical workers, their jobs also played a significant role in their social identity.

NOTES

1. Elyce J. Rotella, *From Home to Office: U.S. Women at Work, 1870-1930* (Ann Arbor, MI: UMI Press, 1981). In Chapter 4, "The Rise of the Clerical Sector," Rotella presents census data that depict the national growth trends in the female clerical labor force; see Tables 4.1-4.3: 62-64.

2. Gretchen Maclachlan, "Women's Work: Atlanta's Industrialization and Urbanization, 1879-1929" ((Ph.D. diss., Emory University, 1992) more closely examines women's work force participation from 1879 to 1920 and concludes that white women worked in a broad stratum of occupations, but were concentrated in manufacturing, increasingly factory labor as the twentieth century progressed, and service occupations, including boarding house keepers and laundry operatives. Laundry work crossed the line from service to manufacturing in the 1920s and was one of the few labors white and black women shared. Clerical labor, Maclachlan notes, greatly expanded white women's occupational choices, but had limited effects on black women's labor. I agree.

3. Rotella, Appendix B, Table B.2, "Average Annual Earnings by Sex in 89 U.S. Cities, 1930". Wage data compiled for the 1930 census indicate that Atlanta clerical workers, both male and female, earned similar or greater annual earnings than manufacturing laborers, although women consistently earned less than their male counterparts in all occupations.These annual earnings composed by the Bureau of the Census tend to more accurately reflect women's real earnings than men's earnings, because the annual earnings were skewed by averaging operative and proprietary or management salaries, which resulted in an overall reduction of male earnings in both clerical and manufacturing occupations.

4. U.S. Department of Commerce. Bureau of the Census. *Fourteenth Census of the United States, 1920: Population*, I, 132.

5. Julia Kirk Blackwelder, "The Mop and the Typewriter: Women's Work in Early Twentieth Century Atlanta" *Atlanta Historical Journal* 27 (Fall, 1983): 24; Rotella, 142, 148.

6. Erickson, "Employment of Women in Offices", 59.

7. U.S. Department of Commerce, Bureau of the Census, *Fourteenth Census of the United States, 1920* (Washington, GPO: 1922), Occupations.

Atlanta, Oakland, and Akron shared comparable population size over the age of ten years, and Atlanta and Oakland shared similarly sized working populations. But proportionately, Atlanta had a larger female work force (37 percent) than Oakland or Akron (23 percent). In Akron, industrial occupations engaged 66 percent of the working population with the female work force concentrated in domestic service and clerical occupations. Oakland engaged nearly 40 percent of its work force industrially with the female work force concentrated in professional service, domestic service, and clerical occupations. Atlanta employed only 28 percent of its work force industrially, with higher female participation rates in clerical, domestic service, and transportation industries.

    8. See Elizabeth M. Lyon "Business Buildings in Atlanta: A Study in Urban Growth and Form" (Ph.D., Emory University, 1971) for a discussion of the development of the commercial city.

    9. The field of female clerical work scholars has grown greatly in the last ten years. Many dissertations consulted in the initial stages of research have been published. Following are some of the most influential American works consulted: Margery Davies, *"Women's Place is at the Typewriter": Office Work and Office Workers, 1870-1930* (Philadelphia: Temple University Press, 1982); Elyce Rotella, *From Home to Office: U.S. Women at Work, 1870-1930* (Ann Arbor: University of Michigan Research Press, 1977); Cindy Sondick Aron, *Ladies and Gentlemen of the Civil Service: Middle Class Workers in Victorian America* (New York: Oxford University Press, 1987); Ileen DeVault, *Sons and Daughters of Labor: Class and Clerical Work in Turn-of-the-Century Pittsburgh* (Ithaca: Cornell University Press, 1990); Lisa M. Fine, *The Souls of the Skyscraper: Female Clerical Workers in Chicago, 1870-1930* (Philadelphia: Temple University Press, 1990; Mary Christine Anderson, "Gender, Class, and Culture: Women Secretarial and Clerical Workers in the United States, 1925-1955, Volume I" (Ph.D. diss., Ohio State University, 1986); and Anita Rapone, "Clerical Labor Force Formation: The Office Woman in Albany, 1870-1930" (Ph.D. diss., New York University, 1981).

    10. For general discussions of the growth of the post-Civil War economy and the development of a permanent white-collar work force see: Harry Braverman, *Labor and Monopoly Capital: The Degradation of Work in the Twentieth Century* (New York: Monthly Review Press, 1974), C. Wright Mills, *White Collar: The American Middle Classes* (New York: Oxford University Press, 1951), Alfred D. Chandler, Jr., *The Visible Hand: The Managerial Revolution in American Business* (Cambridge: Harvard University Press, 1977), and David Gordon, Richard Edwards and Michael Reich, *Segmented Work, Divided Workers: The Historical Transformation of Labor in the U.S.* (Cambridge: Cambridge University Press, 1982).

11. Winifred D. Wandersee, *Women's Work and Family Values, 1920-1940* (Cambridge: Harvard University Press, 1981), 59, 75; Scharf, *To Work and to Wed*, x-xii, 60-61.

12. Wandersee, *Women's Work and Family Values*, 59-60.

13. C. Wright Mills, *White Collar: The American Middle Classes*, (New York: Oxford University Press, 1951), 241, 249, 297.

14. Ileen A. DeVault, "Sons and Daughters of Labor: Class and Clerical Work in Pittsburgh, 1870s-1910s" (Ph.D. diss., Yale University, 1985), 5-7, 14.

15. Harry Braverman, *Labor and Monopoly Capital*, 293.

16. David Lockwood, *The Blackcoated Worker: A Study in Class Consciousness* (London: Ruskin House, 1958); Gregory Anderson, *Victorian Clerks* (Manchester: Manchester University Press, 1976); C. Wright Mills, *White Collar*; Anita Rapone, "Clerical Labor Force Formation: The Office Woman in Albany, 1870-1930" (Ph.D. diss., New York University, 1981); Ileen A. DeVault, "Sons and Daughters of Labor: Class and Clerical Work in Pittsburgh, 1870s-1910s" (Ph.D. diss., Yale University, 1985); Grace Hutchins, *Women Who Work* (New York: International Publishers, 1934).

17. Lockwood, *Blackcoated Worker*, p.34.

18. Anderson, *Victorian Clerks*, p.126.

19. Grace Hutchins, *Women Who Work*, 256.

20. Ibid., 257.

21. Mary Anderson, "The Clerical Worker and Industrial Change" *American Federationist* (September, 1932): 1024.

22. Ibid, 1025.

23. Grace L. Coyle "Women in Clerical Occupations" *Annals of the American Academy of Political and Social Science* 143 (May, 1929); quoted in Davies, *Women's Place is at the Typewriter*.

24. Scharf, *To Work and to Wed*, 23-26, 36-37.

25. Scharf, *To Work and to Wed*, 65, 139-140, 147.

26. Wandersee, *Women's Work and Family Values*, 54.

27. Marie Cooper, interview by author, Tape recording, Atlanta, Georgia, 5 August 1989.

CHAPTER 2

A Manageable Workforce: Scientific Management and Women Workers

In 1916, the *City Builder* proudly boasted that "the character of the city . . . was the reflection of the average businessmen's outlook on life."[1] When the *City Builder* published this declaration, the city was in a transitional stage. In the post-World War I period, Atlanta's economy and its workforce reflected a decidedly white-collar hue. During the 1920s and 1930s, the terms businessman and businesswoman became synonymous with white professionals, entrepreneurs, and white-collar workers. From 1910 to 1940, the manufacturing workforce remained stable, while financial, commercial, and clerical employment grew.

White-collar work opportunities greatly expanded in the city largely because of an underemployed pool of potential women workers. In 1910, manufacturing occupations engaged approximately 12 percent of all employed females, and because of southern occupational segregation this workforce was predominantly white. White-collar female occupations, composed primarily of clerical workers, telephone and telegraph operators, teachers, and nurses, engaged 8.9 percent of all laboring women. Again, white women dominated these positions. By 1930, factory and non-factory manufacturing occupations employed 6.7 percent of all working women. But clerical occupations alone engaged 19.6 percent of all employed females. Changes in the way employers organized office work and whom they employed accompanied the dramatic rise in white-collar female employment.

Atlanta businessmen responded to this occupational change by turning to scientific management techniques. These employers, influenced by the popularized efficiency claims of industrial management science, greatly altered office work patterns. Females entering offices witnessed business efficiency first-hand. This transformation, characterized by task division, low wages, routinization, and occupational stagnation coincided with increasing female clerical employment. Although these techniques affected both male and female office workers, women's office work opportunities rarely extended beyond the low-level positions most affected by scientific management.

Gender issues also greatly influenced women's clerical employment. Marital status, age, and domestic responsibilities often determined whether a woman would be employed and in what capacity. These issues significantly diminished women's ability to expand beyond low-level white-collar occupations. Female clerical workers during the 1920s and the 1930s often performed the most routine, monotonous duties associated with streamlined office methods. Employers judiciously determined that women belonged in low-level positions because their workforce tenure was short-lived. For many women, clerical work posed a difficult dilemma. Enlarging occupational choices afforded women opportunities for economic independence, but domestic roles prevailed as the socially acceptable livelihood for women. "If you are a working girl," one journalist observed, "don't you think, 'Oh, if I had a good husband, children, and a home, I'd be perfectly happy!' The young wife and mother sees the businesswoman and says 'My, think how free she is. Only herself and her pretty clothes to think of.' And she envies you mightily."[2] Employers exploited this rivalry and shaped the malleable female workforce to their needs.

Prevailing labor standardization practices created many office environments that were rigidly defined by tasks. Yet, some businessmen personalized their labor policies utilizing metaphors of family hierarchies that softened the impersonal nature of management efficiency. Businessmen often described women's office roles with terms like loyalty and service, but rarely provided true occupational incentives for long-term service. Women's business occupational achievement never extended much beyond clerical duties. Some women with long-term service achieved considerable status, as supervisors or professionals, but most women remained in low-level clerical positions.

Businessmen's rhetoric on the opportunities available in offices rarely described women's experiences.

Female clerical work changed considerably between 1910 and 1930. Women's office workforce participation rose aided by technological innovations and the retooling of labor force management. In 1910, clerical occupations engaged 8 percent of Atlanta's employed females. By 1930, clerical work engaged nearly 20 percent of the Atlanta female workforce, representing a great occupational expansion for white females in twenty years. Women's clerical labor enlarged businesses' capacity to compete and stimulated the application of nascent employment management techniques.

LABOR MANAGEMENT AND WOMEN WORKERS

Businessmen established, through national associations and personnel policy, standards for managing the office workforce. Many office standardization techniques, characterized by task division, departmentalization, and a subsequent lack of promotional opportunities, rapidly followed the Civil War. Large-scale businesses and government offices applied these techniques prior to widespread female employment, thus effecting change in clerical labor primarily performed by men.[3] Between 1910 and 1930, men still occupied most office positions, but because women supplied the balance of labor, office work hierarchies began to shift along gender lines. Standardization measures removed the promotional vehicle, typically a personal relationship between a boss and employee, utilized by male office workers to rise out of the clerk class. Women's entry into the office certainly eliminated some work opportunities for men, particularly entry-level clerical work. However, with women available to fill the lowest positions within a stable clerk class, fewer men performed low-level clerical work. The extraordinary increase of female clerical workers after World War I lends credence to arguments that women's workforce participation redefined the twentieth-century office.

Standardization measures have a complicated origin, and scholars disagree on how widespread certain management techniques were in the United States. Standardization evolved because with enlarged office staffs, managers cried out for rationalized hiring practices; measuring employee work performance, amid multiplying tasks, required quantification and units of performance; and cost-accounting necessary to insuring company profit further demanded organized operating methods. Standardization measures varied considerably based on firm size and work volume and to some degree, personal management style. Popularly called scientific management, rationalized labor manipulation found greatest ascendancy in large firms. Typically, the rationalized office distributed work by dividing discrete tasks among specialized divisions or departments. Routinization of work, through repetitive tasks and reliance on mechanization, also characterized rational labor management. Finally, homogenization, that is, creating a workforce that shared work tasks, class, gender, or even ethnicity, accompanied many standardization efforts. Although these terms have diverse meanings, they all influenced the office worker by limiting the kind of work performed by an individual. Standardization and rational office management intended to minimize personal interaction between management and the worker and limit the skills necessary to perform the required labor.

The term scientific management gained popularity among office managers initially in the 1910s and continued well into the 1930s. W.H. Leffingwell, president of the National Association of Office Managers, in 1929 described the four eras of office management. The earliest, the Copy Press Era, characterized the period when business records were kept on ledgers and in journals. Leffingwell estimated that the Copy Press Era lasted until approximately 1900. At that time, the Systems Era began. This period, launched with the founding of *System* magazine, promoted orderly and systematic record keeping utilizing card filing cabinets with numerical and alphabetized indexes. *System* served as a promotional mouthpiece for the Shaw Walker Company, the maker of card filing cabinets. The Machine Era followed in 1910 and continued until World War I ended. This era increased the use of "system" and encouraged mechanization to simplify work. Finally, the Era of Scientific Management combined the accumulated techniques of past eras and applied them to personnel management, record keeping procedures, and the routine use of machines.[4]

By the 1920s, systematic labor management was already the norm. Women employed as clerical workers entered offices managed as closely akin to a factory line as commerce allowed. However, office managers conceded that only large concerns hiring hundreds of clerical workers could operate within rigid systematic procedures. Smaller offices adopted the philosophy of scientific management, but their limited staffs could hardly accommodate the minute task division and managerial hierarchy characteristic of scientifically managed offices. "There is only a very limited proportion of offices which may be said to be scientifically organized and managed," Leffingwell conceded, "though a very large proportion use many of the mechanisms of scientific management."[5] Procedures endemic to rational office management, such as time and motion studies, piece work and bonus systems, and centralized personnel offices, required large enough output volumes and staffs to rationalize the costly implementation processes. The philosophic application of scientific management, like the output of smaller office staffs, is much harder to quantify than outright rationalization measures.

Scientific management was not developed with office work in mind. It emerged, approximately in 1895, among a group of engineers in metal-working and steel companies, who desired effective cost measurements and systematic completion of orders. Frederick Taylor, an industrial engineer, presented a paper that proposed scientifically assessing industrial output by studying time and motion of factory labor and measuring the resulting output. Previously, cost projections and savings measures among industrial firms relied on past performance, not the examination of current labor manufacturing rates. Taylor developed a method that allowed management to devise standard time and output measurements for factory line workers. Managers set quotas from which production could be accurately assessed and planned. These techniques spawned a new class of employment, mid-level management.[6] Foremen and factory operatives carried out ideas and standards for work output created by managers. Although earlier mechanization and associated streamlined procedures had reduced operative initiative, scientific management further diminished what little control workers possessed over the cadence of work.[7]

"Taylor always had in mind the development of scientific management in the office," wrote King Hathaway, a Taylor associate, "but except as it was done incidentally in establishing the methods of planning, stockkeeping, purchasing, accounting and so forth, it is one of the many things neither Taylor nor his early associates ever got around to."[8] Taylor's ideas affected office work most profoundly by reducing the scope of work performed by the individual. By the 1920s, most office workers performed specific tasks that offered little opportunity of understanding the business' total operation and that significantly reduced promotional opportunities that went beyond clerical work.

Within their professional organizations, businessmen fluently spoke the language of efficiency. In 1919, the National Association of Office Managers (NAOM) formed and characterized itself as "an association to promote a free exchange of ideas on office management, and to initiate and effect scientific methods of office organization and management." Leading scientific managers, like Leffingwell, presented papers at annual association meetings and facilitated roundtable discussions among business managers. Roundtable sessions produced dialogue concerning applied techniques. In theory, all managers agreed that offices needed to quantitatively measure clerical work tasks and develop standards or quotas to ensure enforcement. At the roundtables, NAOM members shared their standardization experiences. Businessmen recommended that time and motion studies precede rational management implementation. Although costly, time and motion studies could increase work volume output and decrease personnel needs. In application, mechanization and the performance of routine tasks multiplied work output per worker; and thus through this efficiency, office staffs could be reduced. Piece work and bonus systems held individuals accountable for their work output and allowed businessmen to substitute base salaries with payment-for-performance wages. Managers employed bonus systems most commonly among low-level clerical workers such as auditing clerks, stenographers in pools, and mail order clerks. Office managers initiated piece work among typists by measuring carriage returns and key strokes with a cyclometer. Ediphone and dictaphone operators performed piece work that paid for translated cylinders or per line of script. Forced into piece work systems, some women resorted to desperate measures to ensure a living wage.

> When they [Metropolitan Life Corporation] first put in the dictaphone, of course, there was the usual resistance towards the use of them by the girls. In the first week, it was established they had not worked out the plan quite right for some of the girls make over thirty dollars per week. They did that by coming in just as soon as the doors were open. In order to get plenty of cylinders they would steal them, put them in their desks and lock them up and then they would stay until the janitors had to throw them out at night.[9]

The B. F. Goodrich Company of Ohio operated a bonus system with no base pay for stenographic, dictating, mimeograph, multigraph, and addressograph workers. Leffingwell applauded the "payment for performance basis" as a proven standardization measure.

The NAOM hoped to promote standardization measures like piece work and bonus systems in all offices, but most members agreed that these procedures were too costly for widespread implementation. Likewise, other standardization techniques, such as centralized personnel departments, training manuals, and rigid departmentalization, required armies of office workers to achieve much success. Simpler techniques, like homogenization, proved more effective for small offices that required some task flexibility among lower level workers.

In the early 1930s, women's labor activists began meeting and addressing the problems faced by female clerical workers. Grace Coyle and Caroline Manning of the National Young Women's Christian Association, Mary Anderson of the Women's Bureau, and Ethel Erickson of the American Federation of Labor met on July 3, 1930, in Washington, D.C. Throughout the 1910s and the 1920s, the organizations these women represented had focused primarily on female industrial employment, where abuses in working conditions, living conditions, and wages were common. Through these efforts, women's industrial working conditions began to improve, albeit slowly. Child labor and home work declined. However, increased labor disputes initiated by many female manufacturing groups during the 1930s indicated widespread worker dissatisfaction and management abuses that resisted reform measures.[10] Throughout the 1920s, businessmen engaging hundreds of female clerical workers enjoyed an employers' honeymoon. Initial social criticisms launched against female office workers and their employers, most vehement prior to World War I, subsided. Retail advertising, romance novels, and advice columns aimed at businesswomen, emerging during the 1920s, signaled a growing acceptance of white-collar women. By the 1930s, women's labor activists began to question the costs of this convivial mood.

At the July 1930 meeting, the conferees probed the economic and social consequences of feminized offices. "When they [female clerical workers] first started," it was noted, "they had to talk of 'salaries' and 'positions' now they are talking of 'jobs' and 'wages'."[11] Wages dominated the conference discussions, particularly the use of piece work and bonuses and the American Management Association's endorsement of these practices. Many women, the activists noted, expected bonuses at year's end but learned that no bonuses were forthcoming; they had been budgeted into the women's yearly salaries.

A clerical worker's real salary, then, could be considerably lower if the bonuses were eliminated, which occurred with irritating frequency. Opposition to these practices rarely surfaced, in part because employer bans on discussions of salaries inhibited women from uniting to seek general salary increases. Some employers who paid inadequate salaries resorted to the pin-money theory: most women workers did not need the income but labored instead for luxuries. The conferees clearly considered this argument passé and blamed the surplus of female clerical labor, especially commercially trained high school girls, and increased office mechanization for low wages. The activists agreed that more study was required before any measures could be taken.[12]

SURVEYING THE CLERICAL WORKFORCE

In 1931, the Women's Bureau of the U.S. Department of Labor launched a study of female clerical workers in seven American cities that included Atlanta, Chicago, New York, Philadelphia, Hartford, Des Moines, and St. Louis. *Women's Bureau Bulletin Number 120*, published in 1934, summarized office work conditions based on the survey data.[13] The study focused on women in the private sector and covered a broad range of employment concerns, primarily offices classed as advertising, banking, insurance, investment, mail order, publishing, and public utilities. In Atlanta, by special request, the scope of the study was extended to include mercantile, manufacturing and distributing, credit-rating, and oil-company offices. The companies ranged from small, privately owned businesses to large, nationwide firms and their branch offices. Ethel Erickson served as the primary investigator in Atlanta and gathered data in April, May, and June 1931 from fifty-seven offices employing white women and two employing black women. The Atlanta survey included more than 3,700 women, approximately 40 percent of the total female clerical workforce in 1930.[14]

The survey definitively illustrates a widespread use of applied scientific management techniques. Atlanta businessmen, like others across the country, adopted aspects of modern office management and tailored these theories to suit the work place. By the 1930s, managers routinely divided labor in offices and relied upon lower level clerical workers to perform a myriad of tasks. This technique, a standard scientific management element, accomplished several goals: it gave the most routine work to the lowest paid worker and it divided office work into standardized tasks. According to median salary rates compiled by the Women's Bureau in Atlanta, "only five occupations—secretary, stenographer, stenographic not specified, cashier or teller, and supervisor—had medians over $100 (monthly), and these occupations together covered only about one-fourth of the women."[15] The remaining clerical positions including, among others, typist, dictating machine operator, correspondent, file clerk, hand bookkeeper, general clerk, bookkeeping, calculating and billing machine operators, and mail order clerk comprised approximately 75 percent of the Atlanta clerical workforce. These positions averaged monthly salaries of $75 to $100. Merchandising clerks (mail order) commonly earned less than $75 per month. Clearly, Atlanta office managers applied scientific management measures especially among the lower level and least paid office positions occupied by women.

Able to streamline office output and employ less-skilled workers at reduced salaries or wages, office managers adopted standardized task division. However, the Women's Bureau found that few small offices employed rationalization techniques strictly. "When the duties of an employee were varied, the practice was to classify by the major job. In small offices there was a tendency to class all the women as stenographers even though they did almost everything but stenography."[16] For example, Stella Brady, hired in 1934 by the Georgia Parent Teacher Association as a typist, performed a variety of tasks. "I was a bookkeeper," she said; "I never had training, but I was the bookkeeper until they hired one. I did special projects; I did typing and I cut stencils."[17] Although women performed multiple tasks, census compilations grouped most female clerical workers in the stenographer and typist categories, which masked the diversity of clerical work.

The Atlanta survey included companies as large as Sears, Roebuck & Company, which retained 707 women in its offices, and as small as Pilgrim Health and Life Insurance Company, a branch office of a black insurance firm, which employed six female clerical workers. Georgia Power, a large electric utility company serving several southeastern states, employed 248 female clerical workers in its Atlanta office on Marietta Street. These women occupied seventeen different clerical positions, although the company classified most workers as general clerks (70 women) and stenographers (58 women). The remaining positions at Georgia Power were defined by machines women used in their work: addressograph, billing machine, comptometer, dictaphone, ditto machine, key punch, and mimeograph operators.[18] These positions required patience, because the tasks performed were routine, often monotonous, and offered little chance of variety from day-to-day. "I have never had so mechanical a job before nor one with so little responsibility—and the experience has been very interesting," a Works Projects Administration administrator performing temporary work remarked, "[n]ow I can imagine how clerks with monotonous work must feel—no wonder they talk all the time . . . ."[19]

Several large firms combined task division and mechanization to increase their productivity while reducing their office staffs and payrolls. Georgia Power routinely utilized standardization techniques in its Atlanta office. In 1912, the company phased out hand bookkeeping, skilled work often reserved for men that required attention to detail and a knowledge of double-entry bookkeeping. Key punch equipment, introduced in offices in the early 1910s, replaced the hand system for posting accounts. At the time of the survey, Georgia Power employed six female clerical workers as key punch operators. The company trained women to do this work, although it is not clear whether men lost positions in this transition or were simply transferred to different work. More importantly, the bookkeeping system was "installed to systematize and standardize (bookkeeping work) as well as to eliminate hand-done detail." The standardization of bookkeeping work also required revising the billing system. The company installed five billing machines (c. 1926) and trained several female employees to operate them. "Gradually, (over a five-year period of time, 1926-1931) more machines have been added as the bookkeeping centralization work grew until now eleven girls are operating billing machines."[20] Banks also commonly employed women as bookkeepers, who operated billing machines exclusively. Ruth Cox worked in a Birmingham bank from 1929 until 1936, and her sole duty was posting the accounts of daily banking transactions.

> [A]t the bank it was those old timey machines, that would sit up high [approximately three feet off the ground]. We typed in the checks, just like a checkbook. You had your balance, then you had your checks, then you had your deposits. [We] did this for every account. My sister and I worked the As down to the Browns in the Bs. You had one sheet for every customer and he had a ledger sheet and the ledger sheet was the permanent record that the bank kept. . . you posted everyday, two times a day, then you had to balance in the afternoon. Ledger and statement had to balance. If we had a

discrepancy, we had to find out who posted the check wrong. We [also] filed the people's checks every morning after you did the day's work before.[21]

Mechanization greatly influenced the segmentation and standardization of office work prior to World War I, but again only the largest firms introduced mechanized tasks. Machines intensified the routine nature of many clerical tasks, lowered required skill levels, and quickened the work pace.[22] Women entered offices in the transitional stage between hand-work and mechanized work, and they experienced the most dramatic changes in office work. Many women considered machines attractive because they added complexity to their work. "I love those [bookkeeping] machines," Ms. Cox recalled, "seems like machines come easy with me." Ms. Cox adapted well to temporary tasks that involved machines. She enjoyed the challenge they offered. "I loved that old telephone thing [switchboard]," she said, "it was fascinating. Course it had all those holes there and of course, you just had about four to six lines coming in and you had to connect the people in those different offices." Mastering machines gave Ruth a strong sense of accomplishment and a skill transferable to other positions. When she applied for a position with the federal government, Ruth practiced for a machine test, knowing she could skillfully master it.[23]

Although machines gave women a chance to employ learned skills, they also limited women's occupational opportunities. Ms. Cox's experience provides a clear example of how banks divided work among male and female employees. With one-and-one-half years of college, Ms. Cox entered a billing clerk position in 1929. She worked behind a row of male tellers in a room with twenty or thirty other women, all posting the daily transactions on customers' accounts. Over five years, she received no salary increase and performed the same duties. No men worked the billing machines of the commercial accounts department. Her supervisors, however, were male.[24]

Generally, only women working in large firms experienced the minute task division and labor segmentation described by Ms. Cox. Yet, numerous Atlanta firms surveyed employed similar labor management techniques. Atlanta had the highest proportion of small offices among the seven cities surveyed by the Women's Bureau.[25] Most Atlanta credit-rating companies had small clerical staffs, generally fewer than fifty women in an office. Credit-rating firms routinely divided clerical labor into specific tasks and paid the lowest clerical salaries. For example, the Southeastern Underwriters Association, a credit-rating firm for insurance companies, employed thirty-six women in clerical capacities and divided the work among twelve positions. The R. G. Dun Company employed thirty women who worked within eight occupational classifications. Retail Credit Company, a large credit-information company with numerous national branch offices, employed 120 women in its Atlanta office and divided the work among nineteen positions. To its credit, the Retail Credit Company also employed ten female senior supervisors, three junior supervisors, a cashier, a librarian, and an employment supervisor position; none classified by the census as clerical.[26] However, most Atlanta firms retained women in a myriad of clerical or other low-level, static positions, such as stenographer, typist, file clerk, general clerk, and machine operator. Many of the classifications were misleading. A stenographer rarely performed only stenographic work; commonly she answered phones, typed, and filed. Atlanta office managers used many scientific management techniques espoused by the NAOM, but modified structured job classifications to suit the individual firm's needs. Atlanta businessmen also hired women in general clerical job categories, thus avoiding the confines of strict task-defined positions. This strategy allowed managers to hire less-than-skilled female workers, train them for firm-specific jobs, and pay them less. Task division worked well in firms with diverse operations whether they were large or small. The common philosophy managers adhered to invariably placed women in low-level positions dominated by mechanized, routine tasks.

David Gordon, Richard Edwards, and Michael Reich suggest, in *Segmented Work, Divided Workers*, that the division of work tasks increased the homogenization of the U.S. workforce between 1870 and World War II.[27] Throughout this era, low-level office and manufacturing occupations required fewer job skills and relied more on repetition, often enhanced by machine use. Companies creating standardized work tasks and homogenous occupational groups deskilled their workforces. To counteract worker dissatisfaction resulting from this deskilling, companies employed artificial divisions and distinctions among jobs thus creating new job ladders. These manipulations intended to distract and diffuse worker backlash against corporate deskilling. Homogenization and deskilling diminished whatever autonomy pre-World War I clerks possessed in their work places, and by the 1920s, clerical work provided little opportunity for occupational advancement.

Companies routinely employed artificial divisions among clerical work positions that only divided a very small occupational pie. Several managers participating in the Women's Bureau survey admitted that clerical positions in their companies offered limited advancement opportunities to females. Among the credit-rating companies employing female workers, salaries were low (30 percent earned less than $75 monthly, another 32 percent earned between $75 and $100 monthly) and the degree of task division was high. Some of these occupational divisions and distinctions were artificial and suggested a diversity that was not present.[28]

Retail stores and mail order concerns employed virtual armies of Atlanta women in numerous low-level tasks that were highly specialized and often routine. In 1930, the John Reed Company, a ready-to-wear apparel mail order firm, employed an all-female office staff of 172 workers. The women worked in thirty-five distinct occupational categories, many of which involved highly monotonous work. For example, addressograph operators placed metal plates, stamped with names and addresses, in an inked press. These imprints served as the customer's mailing label. Women also performed single tasks such as mail opening, mail reading, label attaching, package opening, longhand addressing, and package weighing for eight hours.[29]

Mechanization and task division were highly correlated among insurance and retail firms. Insurance companies, banks and financial institutions, and retail concerns, primarily mail order, employed the largest numbers of female clerical workers and routinely divided tasks among them. Companies applauded the benefits of increased output accomplished by office mechanization but failed to recognize and compensate for the additional work burdens placed upon their clerical workforces. Typically, mechanization did not replace office workers, but increased their work. Royal Insurance installed dictaphones in 1921; these "dictaphones never replaced anyone, but made for better efficiency, contributing to the gradual growth of the business." Likewise, the installation of three Hollerith tabulating machines did not replace anyone, "but [the company is] constantly putting more and more work into the machine." The Atlanta branch office of the Hartford Fire Insurance Company found dictaphones unsatisfactory and discontinued their use after twelve years. However, the company intended to install Ediphones, which promised new features, and noted that "probably about half of our stenographers will leave and we shall have to hire Ediphone operators, for we only need typists for them."[30]

Some companies found other positions for female workers displaced by office mechanization. The progressive personnel policies of Atlanta Life Insurance Company, owned and operated by Alonzo Herndon, a former slave, stood out among Atlanta companies. Herndon's company retained four female clerical workers displaced by the installation of a Hollerith tabulating machine. However, several other insurance concerns divided the tasks of their female office workers to incorporate the part-time use of machines into existing duties. The Hartford Accident and Indemnity Company introduced four transcribing machines in 1930, and "the stenographers swung over to the part-time use of these machines; there were no resignations or new employees hired."[31]

Because mechanization and standardization were intended to reduce operating expenses, low wages for female clerical workers became the focus of the Women's Bureau study. Male managers attending the NAOM proceedings during the 1920s spoke appreciatively of reducing company expenses through scientific management techniques, including mechanization, piece work, and task division. The bureau investigated personnel records and company payrolls and sent questionnaires to working women, specifically through YWCA summer camps. The Women's Bureau tabulated clerical work compensation levels and sought to determine how factors such as education, training, age, and experience influenced salaries. Wages varied considerably among office concerns, depending on firm size and the degree of task division. Offices that employed large numbers of women in stenographic and typing pools often resorted to piece work. Both NOMA and the American Management Association encouraged the adoption of piece work where it was applicable. As a result, some female typists measured their salaries by the number of lines typed, or the number of inches or strokes completed. NOMA managers complained that women hoarded dictaphone cylinders in their desks to assure bonuses, or simply a living wage, for themselves.

Several factors encouraged office managers to implement piece work practices in the late 1920s and the early 1930s. Women's wages in office work were affected by outdated pin-money theories. These theories assumed that young girls working in offices did not support themselves solely upon their wages and therefore could survive on piecework wages. In addition, by 1930, the combination of increased enrollments in public high school business courses and the proliferation of commercial schools rapidly created an abundance of workers trained for low-level clerical positions. The Women's Bureau noted that these positions, particularly typing and stenography, had already reached saturation levels.[32] Competition between currently employed female clerical workers and young high school graduates seeking office positions afforded little realistic hope of correcting wage discrepancies among clerical workers or challenging the techniques employed by management to reduce wages and increase output. To avoid any potential conflicts concerning wages, business firms often banned discussion of wages among office employees. Margery Davies concludes that management encouraged competition among workers to thwart solidarity and potential labor organization. Management rewarded certain individuals with additional piece work or bonus work, forcing employees to compete for this work among themselves.[33]

Atlanta companies commonly divided tasks and mechanized female office work in the mid-1930s. However, piece work rates did not apply in any of the Atlanta offices surveyed. Two retail establishments, Rich's and Davison-Paxon (later Macy's), and the John Reed Company implemented bonuses or task work systems among their female clerical employees. These earning devices only supplemented regular salaries and generally applied to billing or credit clerks who detected billing errors. All the companies paid their female employees straight salaries computed on a weekly, bi-weekly, or monthly basis. However, this payment method did not ensure good wages. Nearly three-quarters of the surveyed female mail order clerks earned less than $75 monthly; 20 percent labored for less than $50 a month. Black female clerical workers earned considerably less than their white counterparts: 88 percent of those surveyed (out of fifty-seven women) earned less than $75 a month.[34]

Compared to female industrial wages, clerical salaries were generous. Most trained clerical workers earned at least $75 monthly. Secretaries, correspondents, and experienced stenographers could earn monthly salaries as high as $150 to $210. However, clerical work positions commonly required higher educational levels than industrial work. Grammar school graduates could expect to perform only general clerk work, such as mail handling, filing, and certain machine operations. In Atlanta, only mail-order houses employed women without some high school education. Typist and stenographer positions required strong spelling, composition, and grammatical skills. Women sought the necessary skills for these positions both in high schools and business schools; approximately 45 percent completed high school. Both stenographers and typists routinely attended business classes at commercial schools (61 and 51 percent respectively.) Secretaries, generally the highest paid female clerical workers, sought schooling beyond high school more often than any other female clerical worker; approximately 36 percent pursued advanced education.[35]

These investments in education affected earnings. Overall, Atlanta's female clerical workforce was well educated in the early 1930s. Forty percent had attended some high school; 37 percent had completed high school; and 13 percent had pursued advanced education. Women with less-than-high-school educations earned less. Median salary rates illustrate the differences: grammar school graduates earned a median of $68 monthly; women who attended high school, but did not graduate, earned a median of $78 monthly (many would later attend commercial business courses); high school graduates earned a median of $84; and those with advanced education earned a median of $94 monthly. However, schooling alone did not determine wage rates.[36]

Age and experience also affected women's salaries. Typically, median salaries rose with age, especially when correlated with higher levels of education. Experience also favorably affected salary rates: women who stayed with firms more than five years, but less than ten, saw increases in their salaries. However, at least ten years' service was required before women doubled their salaries. Fewer than 12 percent of the women surveyed remained in office work more than ten years. Thirty percent stayed five years, but less than ten. For employers, investment in higher salaries for women was negligible, because most women did not continue working past five years.[37]

Women left their jobs for many reasons. Some were personal, such as illness, marriage, home duties, or a desire for change; twenty percent sought better occupational opportunities and, occasionally, they found it.[38] Ruth Cox worked in Birmingham as a young woman in two different jobs. She came to Atlanta in 1941 to take a federal job, which offered stability and assured advancement in a merit system. Ethel Evans worked as a bookkeeping supervisor for Fulton National Bank but felt that clerical positions experienced high turnover rates, because "the salaries were not adjusted often enough, even though they often changed jobs. Many of them were just girls."[39]

Compared to other types of women's work, particularly industrial and manufacturing positions and teaching, clerical work offered steady employment at predictable salaries. Because piece work did not apply in Atlanta, a stenographer or typist could depend on a set weekly wage. By contrast, Atlanta teachers suffered greatly because the city had borrowed during the 1920s to maintain an adequate education budget, and by the early 1930s it was forced to reduce teacher salaries. Although many Atlanta concerns dismissed female clerical workers because of the Depression, these reductions mostly occurred early in 1930. By the time of the survey, in 1931, companies relied on limited staffs, but continued to reduce their workforces by attrition. Women seeking occupational advancement during the 1930s experienced great difficulty because high unemployment permitted companies to indulge in conservative hiring practices and subjective personnel policies.[40]

Atlanta firms utilized many scientific management techniques involving labor segmentation and work division, but they commonly avoided establishing centralized personnel departments and objective personnel standards.[41] Age discrimination affected female clerical workers more profoundly than any other gender issue. Age is identified as a gender issue because employers repeatedly linked age with personal appearance and female work traits. Very few employers positively associated maturity with female clerical worker ability. Managers used phrases such as, "young and good looking" and "young and temperate" to describe desired female employment traits. The Atlanta Gas Light Company, which employed fifty-one women, replied to a question regarding age restrictions by stating that "young and good looking" women were preferred. The Commercial Credit Company expressed similar sentiments. The Sinclair Refining Company described itself as "a young organization; [that] plans to hire [women] between the ages of twenty and thirty." The company auditor continued, "women over thirty are trained in the other man's way." Only one employer, the *Atlanta Constitution*, expressed a preference for older women. The interviewer noted that "several women over fifty [were] seen in the building, [but the] others looked fairly young."[42]

It is no wonder that the term "girls" was widely used to describe female office workers. Most offices hired women immediately out of high school or from business schools and office machine company training programs. Many women employed as clerical workers, approximately 50 percent, failed to complete high school, although most Atlanta firms preferred some high school training. The Women's Bureau calculated that women between twenty and twenty-five years of age composed nearly 40 percent of the working women surveyed.

Women under thirty made up another 25 percent. Nearly 10 percent had not celebrated their twentieth birthday.[43] "When registering at the Post Office, Community Employment Bureau and the regular business employment bureaus, they require you to give your age," one elderly business woman recalled. "As soon as you give it, if you are honest, that is the end for you, as all calls for office help of any kind are for 'Young girls about twenty-five years of age, college education, five or six years experience, etc.'"[44] Age restrictions significantly narrowed employment possibilities for Atlanta women seeking work during the Depression.

Marital status also affected women's opportunities in offices. Businessmen released married women, or did not hire them, for many reasons. Most commonly, businessmen blamed the dire economic times. The city joined the fray when, in 1932 and 1935, members of the Atlanta Board of Education suggested a ban on married female teachers. Both measures failed to pass. Their intent, however, was clear. Married female workers competed for jobs with single or married men and single women. Nevertheless, the Women's Bureau survey recognized a certain leniency among Atlanta firms toward employing married women. Of the women surveyed, 68 percent were single, 26 percent were married, and 6 percent were widowed, separated, or divorced. These percentages mirrored the marital status of all Atlanta clerical workers.[45] Yet, twenty-five firms enforced employment policies that discriminated against married women. Eighteen firms hired single women exclusively; and if marriage occurred, thirteen of these businesses would allow employment to continue. This type of liberalism was not expected by women office workers, who anticipated that business practices would reflect the more conservative societal norm.

Several firms, including Southern Bell, Western Union, and Western Electric, barred the hiring and retention of married women workers. The reasons for this policy were never clearly stated. The Retail Credit Company also did not hire married women and systematically released women who married. "Unless a girl's record is entirely satisfactory and there is some good reason for retaining her," a 1934 Manager's Manual stated, "the best handling is to make good with a girl who is getting married, and drop her. In exceptional instances, it might be satisfactory for a girl to remain with us after marrying, provided she can continue working up to full capacity without being under strain."[46] The strains of marriage, the company believed, stemmed from her domestic situation and the additional household duties marriage demanded. Domestic roles, for single as well as married women, played an important part in their employment at Retail Credit Company. "It is especially desirable that girls live at home," the 1935 Manager's Manual stated. "It should be ascertained, however, whether they have any housework to look after regularly. Experience has shown this taxes a girl too much for her to get the best results in her work."[47]

Clearly, as some employment policies demonstrated, marriage presented a serious obstacle to Atlanta women seeking or engaged in clerical work. Yet, married women's clerical employment increased between 1920 and 1940. In 1920, married women composed approximately 19 percent of the female clerical workforce; single women made up the remaining 80 percent. By 1930, married women's clerical workforce participation had risen to 26 percent and grew throughout the Depression. By 1940, married women comprised approximately 37 percent of the female office workforce, an increase of 11 percent. Although many employers prohibited hiring or keeping married women workers, these clerical workers continued to seek and keep their jobs. These figures suggest two possibilities: that employers did not rigidly abide by employment standards, especially during the Depression when retaining experienced workers was more profitable than training new workers, or that some women concealed their marriages to keep their jobs.

Despite many employers' preference for single women, the Women's Bureau felt that married women experienced less discrimination in Atlanta, and the southeast in general, than in the other cities surveyed. In Richmond, a 1940 Women's Bureau survey revealed that married women constituted 28 percent of the city's clerical workforce. In Chicago, New York, and Philadelphia, married female clerical workforce participation remained low, between 10 and 17 percent.[48] Comparatively, married women fared better in Atlanta and Richmond. Despite these statistics, the experience of married Atlanta women seeking clerical work was not all positive. Nor was married women's employment condoned by the entire Atlanta community. One outspoken critic was Methodist Bishop Warren A. Candler. In 1937, Candler addressed the graduating class of the Georgia State College for Women in Milledgeville and advised women not to endanger their femininity by engaging in politics and business. The bishop urged women to remain in their homes. Yet, the Christian Council, an interdenominational ministers' group composed of approximately 120 churches, never commented on white-collar working wives. It focused instead on wayward women, primarily industrial laborers, prostitutes, and the unemployed.[49] A female columnist in the *Atlanta Journal* described the entrance of married women into business and the professions as the "Anglo-Saxon riddle." The author applauded women's business acuity but urged wives to set aside fifteen to twenty years to raise a family. Mildred Seydell, a columnist for the Atlanta *Georgian*, argued that "women are learning to be good wives and mothers and businesswomen at one and the same time."[50]

Married and single working women also advocated women's right to business success. Miss Maybelle G. Jones, an editor for the Retail Credit Company house organ, felt women's skills meshed well with editing tasks. "Their business cares, however, seem not to interfere with the domestic work," she argued, "and each one of them—dentist or lawyer or architect or engraver—is vitally interested in her home." Ironically, Miss Jones married while employed at Retail Credit Company and had to resign. However, not all women supported working wives. Mrs. Gussie B. Ivey, a contractor, went into business for herself after her children were grown. "My most unpleasant rebuffs," she recalled, "came from women with whom I had associated before I went into business." One woman wrote to Seydell, in 1930, requesting the columnist's help. "Won't you please write something in favor of married women's working?," she pleaded. "Everyone seems to be so prejudiced against married women in favor of single women. If anything, should it not be just the other way around?" The young woman signed herself "Anxious."[51]

For a young married or single woman struggling to make ends meet, or an older woman seeking to reenter the workforce, the subjective nature of employers' personnel policies could be unsettling. Women's positions in offices, while relatively stable once secured, were subject to some gender-specific qualifications. Physical appearance played an important role for women seeking clerical jobs. Rich's, a department store, hired women as salesclerks and in many clerical positions. In a tale of "Three Girls" in the company newspaper, the personnel manager declined hiring the women primarily based on physical appearance: too much make-up, dirty hair, untidy clothes, and a bad complexion. This moralistic piece urged women to "see the company nurse if you feel that your personal appearance is a result of illness, or lack of understanding."[52] The Retail Credit Company also urged attention to appearance and showcased new female employees in the company newspaper. For example, when Margaret Brooks graduated from the Georgia School of Technology Evening School the Retail Credit Company newsletter noted that she was "one of the attractive girls of the Home Office Statistical Department." Captions of female clerical workers' photographs commonly described the women as attractive, regardless of the activity or event reported. Anniversary notices of female employees rarely outlined their work histories, but focused on their loyalty, appearance, and temperate personalities[53] Some women felt that appearance was not extraordinarily important but believed that female clerical workers merely observed the era's rules of decorum.[54]

DEFINING THE OFFICE

Scientific management techniques, widely interpreted and broadly applied, significantly affected the work environment of Atlanta female office workers. Atlanta offices did not rigorously apply scientific management, but the techniques they applied affected low-level workers, many of them women. Men and women who worked in offices between 1910 and 1930 experienced dramatic changes in the ways they performed their work and in the authority hierarchies that evaluated and regulated their work. Expanded managerial positions created an intermediate level for male clerks to aspire to. Few women clerical workers could or did. For male office workers, the opportunities may not have been any more expansive, but the ability to rise still existed, despite the loss of autonomy inherent in task division, mechanization, and labor-management segregation

As noted, small firms did not apply the segmentation and rationalization techniques of scientific management, and these businesses probably retained personalized work relationships at all levels. Even large firms maintained atmospheres of warmth and congeniality among the employers and employees; people would not voluntarily subject themselves to cold and inhuman work lives if alternatives existed. However, the large firms did use centralized personnel offices, divided tasks into least denominators, and employed management hierarchies that relatively few employees could enter, especially women. The following case study discusses how a growing Atlanta firm used scientific management techniques to enlarge its business capacity and manage its employees.

NOTES

1. *City Builder*, I (June 1916), 7; as quoted in Charles Garofalo, "Business Ideas in Atlanta, 1916-1935" (Ph.D. diss., Emory University, 1972), 46.

2. "Blue Bird," *Inspection News* 17 (March 1932): 41.

3. Davies, *Women's Place*, 28-29; Aron, *Ladies and Gentlemen*, 5.

4. W.H. Leffingwell, "The First Half Century of Office Management" *Proceedings of the National Association of Office Managers, Tenth Annual Conference, 1929*, 11.

5. Leffingwell, 11.

6. Chandler, 274-276. Chandler fully explores the application of rational management and standardization techniques among the railroads, an industry so large and diffuse that operating without these measures it could not meet minimum criteria, such as train schedules.

7. Harry Braverman, *Labor and Monopoly Capital: The Degradation of Work in the Twentieth Century* (New York: Monthly Review Press, 1974), 119; Davies, 127; and Weiss, 66.

8. Leffingwell, 13.

9. F. E. Barth, Roundtable Discussions, *Proceedings of the National Association of Office Managers Fourth Annual Conference, Detroit, Michigan 14-16 June 1923*, 45.

10. There are numerous scholarly works that detail labor and management disputes during the 1930s. Women engaged in southern manufacturing industries played pivotal roles in these disputes. For example see, Jacqueline Dowd Hall, et. al., *Like a Family: The Making of a Southern Cotton Mill World* (Chapel Hill: University of North Carolina Press, 1987) and Julia Kirk Blackwelder, *Women of the Depression: Caste and Culture in San Antonio, 1929-1939* (College Station: Texas A & M University Press, 1984).

11. Margaret Williamson, Executive Secretary of National YWCA Business and Professional Department to Mary Anderson, Director Women's Bureau, TL, 6 November 1930, Correspondence 1930, RG 69, National Archives.

12. Ibid.

13. Ethel Erickson, *Women's Bureau Bulletin 120*, "Employment of Women in Offices" (Washington, D.C.: G.P.O., 1934).

14. U.S. Works Projects Administration, Planning Projects, Clerical Work Surveys 1935-1937, RG 69, File 217, National Archives, Washington, D.C. The survey summarized employment conditions among female office workers and focused on the use of machines, personnel policies, education levels,

promotional opportunities, vacations, and other benefits. The Women's Bureau filled out questionnaires based on interviews with company managers, and these documents are the only extant primary source. Some data, pertaining to salary rates, occupational grouping, schooling, type of office, experience, and age, were gathered and analyzed, but the actual data are not available. It is important to note that the survey interviewers relied on management responses to the majority of the questions posed regarding working conditions; thus a bias should be interpreted into the data. These managers likely refrained from disclosing information that could tarnish their company's image. However, some responses were candid. For example, one commercial loan company manager listed "young and good looking" as a job requirement. Subsequent references to information gather from the survey form will be cited as: Atlanta Clerical Work Survey, General Interview, [company name].

15. Erickson, 56.

16. Ibid, 5.

17. Stella Brady, Interview by author, 21 April 1987.

18. Atlanta Clerical Work Survey, General Interviews, Sears Roebuck & Company, Pilgrim Life Insurance Company, and Georgia Power.

19. Louise Leonard McLaron, Director of the Southern Summer School for Women Workers, Arnold, Maryland, to Mary Barker, Georgia Chairman, Committee on Workers' Education, ALS, 11 December 1933. McLaron accepted a two-week temporary job with the Bureau of Labor Statistics to supplement her income and to help her understand the clerical worker.

20. Atlanta Clerical Work Survey, General Interview, Georgia Power.

21. Mrs. Ruth Cox, interview by author, Tape recording, Atlanta, Georgia, 19 January 1992.

22. Davies, *Women's Place*, 37.

23. Ms. Ruth Cox, interview by author, Tape recording, 19 January 1992.

24. Ibid.

25. Erickson, 13.

26. Atlanta Clerical Work Survey, General Interviews, Southeastern Underwriters Association, R. G. Dun Company, and Retail Credit Company.

27. David Gordon, Richard Edwards, and Michael Reich, *Segmented Work, Divided Workers: The Historical Transformation of Labor in the U.S.* . (Cambridge: Cambridge University Press, 1982).

28. Erickson, 55.

29. Atlanta Clerical Work Survey, General Interview, John Reed Company.

30. Atlanta Clerical Work Survey, General Interviews (Insurance), Royal Insurance Company, Hartford Accident and Indemnity Company, U. S. Fidelity

and Guaranty Company, Cotton Insurance Company, Fire Company's Adjustment Bureau, Hartford Fire Insurance Company, Fireman's Fund Insurance Company, Travelers Insurance, Crum and Forster, America Fire, A. H. Turner, Aetna, American Foreign Insurance Company, Industrial Life and Health Insurance Company, Pilgrim Health and Life Insurance Company, and Atlanta Life Insurance Company; General Interviews (Retail, Mail Order, and Mercantile), Sears Roebuck and Company, Keely Company, J. M. High, J. P. Allen, Davison Paxon Company, Southeastern Express Company, John Reed Company, Southern Grocery Stores, Great Atlantic and Pacific Tea Company, and Rich's Incorporated.

31. Atlanta Clerical Work Survey, General Interviews, Atlanta Life Insurance Company and Hartford Accident and Indemnity.

32. Williamson to Anderson, 6 November 1930, Correspondence 1930, RG 69, National Archives.

33. Davies, *Women's Place*, 173.

34. Erickson, 55.

35. Ibid, 60-61.

36. Ibid, 56-58.

37. Ibid, 61-62.

38. Ibid, 62.

39. Ms. Ruth Cox, interview by author, 19 January 1992; Ms. Ethel Evans, interview by author, Tape recording, 8 February 1992.

40. Atlanta Clerical Work Survey, General Interviews.

41. Erickson noted in her summary that centralized personnel relations, manifest either in a separate employment office or limited to the duties of one person, were preferable because they tended to limit subjective decisions based on nonjob-related qualifications. Given this definition, forty out of the fifty-five offices surveyed reported centralized employment operations. However, among banking and loan, utilities, credit and insurance rating, and manufacturing and distribution companies, the majority did not utilize centralized employment offices. Typically, department heads or managers determined who would be hired. Exceptions to this general rule were Retail Credit Company, Southern Bell, Georgia Power, Sears Roebuck, and Davison-Paxon, operated by R. H. Macy of New York. These firms stated that employment departments accepted applications, but it is not clear if the decision to hire was made through standard criteria. Even a large firm like Gulf Refining Company, which employed 151 women in their offices, allowed office managers to choose their employees, based on "morals and education." Erickson, 63. Atlanta Clerical Work Survey, General Interview, Gulf Refining Company.

42. Atlanta Clerical Work Survey, General Interviews, Atlanta Gas Light Company, Commercial Credit Company, Sinclair Oil Refining Company, and the Atlanta Constitution, 1934, RG 69, National Archives.

43. Erickson, 59.

44. Julia Kirk Blackwelder, "Quiet Suffering: Atlanta Women in the 1930s" *Georgia Historical Quarterly* (Summer 1977), 115.

45. Erickson, 62. The census figures for 1930 show married women as 27 percent of the clerical work force, 62 percent being single, and 11 percent widowed, divorced, or separated.

46. "Manager's Manual," September 1934, TMs, Equifax Library, Atlanta, Georgia.

47. Retail Credit Company, "Manager's Manual" (December 1935) TMs, Equifax Library, Atlanta.

48. Women's Bureau, "Office Work and Office Workers in 1940" *Women's Bureau Bulletin No. 188*, Richmond Survey, 59; Erickson, "Employment of Women in Offices" *Women's Bureau Bulletin No. 120*, Chicago Survey, 1931, New York City Survey, 1930-31, Philadelphia Survey, 1931, 29, 46-47, 84.

49. Christian Council of Atlanta, Evangelical Ministers Association Papers, Minutes April 1926-March 1938, Atlanta Historical Society Library.

50. Blackwelder, "The Mop and the Typewriter," 27; "Can a Woman Have a Career and Home?," *Atlanta Journal*, 7 January 1923, 11.

51. Frank Daniel, "Atlanta Women Have Man-Sized Jobs," *Atlanta Journal Sunday Magazine*. 24 August 1924, 7; "Anxious" to Mildred Seydell, 17 October 1930, TL, Seydell Collection, Special Collections, Woodruff Library, Emory University, Atlanta.

52. Richard A. Rich Papers, Store Publications, *Rich Bits* 14 January 1927, 6, Special Collections, Emory University Library, Atlanta.

53. *Roundtable* (August 1939, 59) .

54. Mrs. Ruth Cox, interview by author, 19 January 1992.

CHAPTER 3

What an Office Should Be

An office is a funny thing: each morning certain men
And certain girls and certain boys come into it again
And hang their coats on certain pegs, their hats on certain hooks,
And sit them down at certain desks in front of certain books,
They all have certain work to do in just a certain time,
Concerning certain dollars for a certain fixed per diem,
And then at just a certain hour, in sunshine or in rain,
They close their desks and hurry out to catch a certain train.
An office is a tragic thing when that is all there is
When each one has his certain work and certain way of his.
And wallows in a certain rut and never seems to see
That there are certain other ones in life as well as he.
For we would find a certain fun in certain other ways,
If we would give a work of cheer on certain busy days—
When problems vex, when certain things require a helping hand,
Would give a certain sympathy that mortals understand.
An office is a pleasant place—at least a certain kind
That has a certain brotherhood where day by day you find
Some neighbor with a new idea he's glad to pass along,
A certain sort of friendliness, a certain sort of song,
There is a certain duty that we owe to other men
To help them when they need a lift, to steady them again.
An office can become in time, to man and girl and boy,
A certain kind of fellowship, and work a certain joy.

Anonymous[1]

Early twentieth century business management aimed to improve office work productivity and maintain stable, satisfied workforces. As managers increasingly employed scientific management methods, work tasks became routine and impersonal. And as the poem suggests, workers often looked for labor satisfaction in each other, not necessarily their work. To offset perceived employee restlessness, employers began to implement a mix of welfare capitalism, paternalism, and scientific management.

Corporate welfare policies emerged prior to World War I. They had been initiated earlier in industrial settings, especially in the large northern manufacturing centers. In the South, corporate welfare policies were most pronounced in textile manufacturing, extractive and heavy industries, and among the railroads. Welfare capitalism practiced by textile manufacturers evokes the most vivid images of paternalistic labor management. These manufacturers frequently implemented policies and practices that controlled as well as benefited workers. By establishing company housing, schools, and stores in the name of philanthropic concern, employers fulfilled social obligations that then allowed them to assuage complaints of deskilling, low pay, and brutal working hours lodged against them by labor unions and social welfare workers. For the employee, the overt measures of paternalism often obscured the most onerous aspects of corporate welfare, particularly the underlying sense of obligation. Employers expected loyalty in return for the material "advantages" they afforded their employees. In the isolated company towns established in the South, these practices inured the workforce to the company and created several generations of a permanent wage-labor class.[2]

Personnel management in offices reflected a new form of paternalism, a far subtler means of control hidden in the folds of scientific management. As later chapters will emphasize, twentieth-century paternalism was endorsed by whole urban communities, and by both male and female citizens. Through a complex mix of urban propaganda (embodied in civicism, morality, social position, and rigid gender roles, a corporate work ethos emerged and claimed economic, moral, and social superiority, despite the often ill-disguised profit motive.

Corporate personnel management among Atlanta firms varied greatly, during the early 1920s, most operated without centralized personnel departments, relying instead on personnel standards developed by individual executives or supervisors. By the 1930s, many larger firms, like Sears Roebuck and Company and Retail Credit Company, both of which employed armies of white-collar workers, had adopted standardized job qualifications; inaugurated training programs; and provided corporate welfare benefits to employees such as medical insurance, paid vacation time, and liberal sick leave. Despite the time and money invested in these standardized policies, managers frequently used subjective, personal management decisions in day-to-day office operations. Scientific management ordered the flow of work, but managers served to personalize the work environment.[3]

At Atlanta's Retail Credit Company, later renamed Equifax, organization-wide scientific management of employees and company operations began in about 1912 and played a substantial role in employer and employee relations throughout the 1930s. The company founders, brothers Cator and Guy Woolford, believed that thoroughly standardized tasks and personnel relations would ensure company profitability and reduce white-collar turnover. Some personnel decisions, however, remained subjective and clearly reflected the owners' personal beliefs concerning morality, social and work conduct, self-improvement, and appropriate gender roles. Utilizing metaphors of family that expressed paternalistic concern for their employees, the Woolfords hoped to offset the ill-effects of standardized work routines. These techniques affected both male and female employees, but frequently limited only female workers' ability to compete beyond prescribed gender roles. Male and female co-workers at Retail Credit Company labored within similar systematic work routines, but women's advancement repeatedly failed to extend beyond "women's place" in business.

THE "SYSTEM" OF MANAGEMENT

In 1899, Cator Woolford, with his younger brother Guy, moved from Chattanooga, Tennessee, to Atlanta to establish a retail credit-reporting agency aptly named the Retail Credit Company. As a retail grocer and active member of the Retail Merchants Association in Chattanooga, Cator Woolford understood the need for a reliable credit-reporting source. Buying the publishing rights of an outdated Atlanta credit-rating book, Woolford launched his own credit-reporting agency in the Gate City. Originally envisioned for use by retail merchants, the credit report became an essential tool in risk selection among insurance companies. Woolford capitalized upon the rapid expansion of life insurance companies and opened a branch office in Dallas, Texas, in 1902. In less than a decade, the Woolfords needed more help and expanded the Atlanta home office to eleven employees. By 1907, Retail Credit Company had opened branch offices in Baltimore, New York, Greensboro, North Carolina, and Philadelphia. In the same year, the company introduced the first product of a scientifically inspired management decision—company instruction manuals.

Cator Woolford lived by the details. Walter C. Hill, a first-tier executive and subsequent Retail Credit president, described his friend and patron:

> Cator Woolford was an intense man . . . . He knew that any end product, whatever its nature and whatever its size, rested on a mass of detail, and that the perfection of the end product . . . depended on the efficiency with which the detail was organized and executed. For an employee to come to the office without his keys, his watch, or money, was not just an awkward bungle but the result of a faulty home practice.[4]

On every desk, employees found instruction manuals that provided detailed job performance standards. By 1915, the company had compiled a manager's manual, a branch office manager's manual, and one for each of the six key occupations within the company: inspector, checker, service reviewer, inquiry clerk, stenographer, and office service clerk. The manuals proliferated as company operations expanded. By the early 1930s, seventeen manuals instructed more than 200 Home Office employees on most tasks they performed.[5]

System became synonymous with management at Retail Credit Company, and the Woolfords applied it to every aspect of company operations. Although job manuals and efficiency methods were often inflexible, the company encouraged employee initiative through a "put-up system." This system encouraged employees to identify weaknesses in their own work operations and then suggest practical solutions. In 1913, Cator Woolford developed a Suggestion Plan that encouraged employees to supply "put-ups" to all aspects of company operations, not simply for their own specific tasks. The plan offered rewards at year's end for the best suggestions. Efficiency pins and clubs appeared in 1912 to reward employee job performance. All these progressive management policies were intended to bolster employee morale, streamline operations, and instill a service-oriented philosophy among employees.

Expanding operations and greatly enlarged office staffs, both in the Atlanta home office and branch offices, impelled the company to reconsider its management policies. In 1933, the Retail Credit Company hired New York-based management consultants H. A. Hopf and Company to study company organization and personnel policies. "The influence of ownership has not yet assumed autocratic aspects," Hopf concluded, "but the possibility of such a development should be recognized and guarded against." At Retail Credit Company, standardization methods had come to dominate company operations largely because of the efforts of Vice-president Guy Woolford, who had an avid personal interest in scientific management theory. Hopf's report concluded that Retail Credit Company suffered from too much system and not enough subjectivity. "More management by personalities and less by mathematics," the report recommended, "would be found to be one of the greatest single boons that the Home Office should confer upon the field." From Hopf's perspective, company executives— namely the Woolford brothers—and several hand-picked managers and long-term employees—Walter Hill, George Bland, and James Malone—negatively influenced company operations through their insistence on scientific management.

Retail Credit Company certainly applied scientific management to the extreme. System appeared regularly in manager manuals, job descriptions, and company publications, especially in the moralistic management editorials commonly found in the early issues of *Inspection News* and the *Roundtable*, the company's two house organs. The *Inspection News Journal*, established in 1916 and later shortened to *Inspection News*, catered to male credit inspectors and the business community that the company served. The *Roundtable*, a popular term used among scientific managers that implied an open forum for ideas, began in 1928 and focused on employee activities but largely refrained from personnel issues and management input. The publication focused on employee anniversaries, weddings, and company picnics in both the home office and the branch offices throughout the country.[6]

Although the company's publications focused on efficiency and output, they also consistently stressed loyalty and service, to the firm and its customers, and implied that long-term service would be rewarded. "We feel, . . . that there is no organization which can give better advancement to young men," a branch manager noted, "as it is a young man's organization almost entirely with the exception of the men who are executives high up . . . ." To reward service, upper management initiated pensions for long-term employees, who were almost always men. Women were largely excluded from pension benefits because they tended to move in and out of the workforce frequently. "Not many of our clerical force will stay with us long enough," operating executive Walter C. Hill wrote, "to get in the pension class . . . ."[7] But there were exceptions. As the 1930s progressed, more women celebrated five-, ten-, and even twenty-year anniversaries with the company. All of these women were single or widowed.

Women working at Retail Credit Company generally filled the lowest level positions, as stenographers, typists, billing clerks, and information clerks. Some women remained in these low-level positions despite ten or fifteen years of service. By far, the majority of female employees remained fewer than five years, presumably in low-level jobs. Women never filled management positions, as defined by the company. Yet throughout the 1930s, a small number of long-term female employees rose to supervise all-female departments such as billing, stenographic, and information.

The *Inspection News* and the *Roundtable* regularly recognized employees promoted to higher positions or those celebrating long-term service. These notices usually consisted of a photograph and a brief career biography. Men generally advanced from field inspectors to administrative positions in the home or branch offices and then on to management. Their anniversary or promotional notices consistently traced their occupational advancement within the company, whereas women's notices rarely outlined the work they performed. Generally the bulletins referred to women as "loyal" and "service-oriented," but provided few details of their jobs. This pattern suggests that most women performed clerical work, and that they did not advance from these positions into the management hierarchy the way male employees could. Even those women clearly serving in supervisory positions received perfunctory anniversary reviews that generally described their temperament, not their career advancement. The word management never appeared in a woman's anniversary notice.[8]

The women who did advance to supervisory positions shared two common traits: they began in low-level clerical positions and rose to supervise all-female employment divisions. In 1912, Mrs. George Halpin joined the Atlanta office, as Miss Mabel Magruder, in a stenographic position. Twenty years later, as a widow, she served as the head of the Organization Division of the Operating Department. Catherine Dorsey, described as "a popular employee," began working at Retail Credit Company in 1917. She rose from general clerical work to a supervisory position in the Billing Department and then to head of the Adjustment Section. Myrtle Adams, on her tenth anniversary, claimed responsibility for the local employment of all female Home Office employees. And Marie Welch, hired for clerical work in the Fee Section of the Records Division, "due to her unusual accuracy, now heads the Billing Section in this division."

Their success, however, did not mirror the experiences of most female clerical employees. Margaret White remained in the home office for fifteen years. "She is a company employee," the *Inspection News* reported, "who, as they say 'has stuck to her post'." She never moved out of a clerical position. Upon serving her tenth year, "Miss Williamson, our Canadian representative" the *Inspection News* noted, "like many of the feminine members of the Company has remained at one post during her entire length of service."[9] For these women, length of service and company loyalty did not ensure any occupational rewards.

Some women achieved positions of considerable authority, albeit within a female sphere. The traditional managerial ladder at Retail Credit Company began with inspectors, an exclusively male position. These men rose through the ranks in the smaller branch offices, which hired small female staffs. Some women employees transferred from branch offices to the home office for the opportunity to rise to supervisory positions because in the small branch offices, women were likely to remain in low-level clerical positions. Turnover in the branch offices was high, especially among the inspector positions. Ambitious men in the branch offices frequently transferred to the home office for mid-level positions such as service reviewer or division supervisor before moving back to the branch offices as managers or assistant managers. Women in the home office who aspired to higher positions had to remain in Atlanta and compete with men from the branch offices; those women who successfully won promotions fought considerable odds.

The chief obstacle to upward mobility among women was marriage. When Walter Hill claimed that few women stayed with the company long enough to collect pensions, it was not because women did not want to stay, but because they were forced to resign upon marriage. Every female employee entering Retail Credit Company understood this stipulation. Although established as a policy among many Atlanta firms, termination upon marriage was ignored or waived if these firms felt an investment would be lost. The rising numbers of married women clerical workers throughout the 1930s confirms this observation. Yet, the Retail Credit Company rigorously enforced the marriage rule, and the female employees accepted this socially condoned occupational hazard.

In many offices, the marriage clause proved to be a particularly effective method of control. Prohibitions against married female office workers achieved two ends: they abided by middle-class social norms that enforced rigid gender roles and they provided an excuse for employers to limit investment in female employees. Industrial concerns, on the other hand, rarely terminated female employees upon marriage. In fact, before effective child labor regulation, companies encouraged the concept of family labor systems. Within the largely middle-class environment of business offices, family labor systems relied on single women or male white-collar workers to contribute to family income.[10]

Retail Credit Company accepted gender roles enforced by class and social values, typified in gender-specific marriage clauses, and also created its own gender stratification by enforcing occupational hierarchies and limitations that controlled women's career opportunities. For example, the company librarian was an exclusively female position, but one that conferred status and considerable responsibility. Until 1926, the Retail Credit Company operated a mandatory library program, in which the librarian assigned reading to employees. The librarian, consulting employee personnel records, determined where personal and professional interests lay for each employee and suggested applicable reading material. The company newspaper insisted that reading requirements did not exist but encouraged every employee to participate. Miss Rix, a seven-year company veteran, remembered, "Those first books, as I recall them, showed, in a general sense, the need for system, method, and loyalty, in order to advance."[11] Clearly, the company library program inculcated employee initiative and adherence to company standards. Upon completing a book, employees wrote a brief comment that verified they had read and understood the book. The comments also assisted the librarian in eliminating topics considered the readers found uninteresting. By 1927, a "book-of-the-month" plan replaced the old system. Every three months a list circulated from which employees chose the books they would read. The librarian noted, "In this way, you will control and choose your own reading." But not whether you wanted to read. Eventually an appointed library board reviewed all books before recommending their addition to the library. With one of her duties substantially reduced, the librarian then became editor of house publications.

The library program was a particularly dynamic way to influence and control employees. This program, like others, was not limited to women but it is significant that the female librarian played a key role in promoting themes of loyalty, service, and duty to the company. It was the librarian's responsibility to enforce the habits of industry gained through reading that the company deemed profitable. This corporate role strikingly paralleled women's roles within the middle-class family: it was the mother's duty to enforced morality and good habits among her children. Having a female as librarian served to soften what could have been perceived as a highly invasive and controlling aspect of company policy.

Another position held by women at the Retail Credit Company also promoted employee loyalty. A succession of female editors directed the two company publications, *Inspection News* and *The Roundtable*. Both publications emphasized the importance of personal and professional self-improvement. The editor actually penned only a few of the moralistic pieces published in the newsletters, but she filled a symbolic role, much like the librarian. As the apparent arbiter of company publications, the editor moderated issues as diverse as company policy and employee concerns. Through appeals to efficiency, she condoned the control of the work process through scientific management. At the same time, the editor wrote and encouraged writing that supported the company's active interest in and influence over employees' personal conduct. One piece intended to reassure the new employee by telling him that the company "took a personal interest in his welfare, not a selfish interest assumed because of the desire to get the most out of the employee . . . . He would discover that the company had an interest in his home, his finances, his insurance, his savings, his investments, his education, and even in the development of his personality." Executive Secretary George Bland believed that corporate responsibility required establishing and enforcing business and personal conduct standards among employees.[12]

Company interest in employee conduct, both personal and professional, stemmed from very practical concerns. Employee attrition at Retail Credit Company, especially in inspector positions, troubled executives. To combat what they perceived as large turnover, company management invested in a group insurance plan, training programs, and stricter hiring practices. Two training programs resulted from an introspective 1926 survey of operating methods; one was for inspectors and the other for managers. To inspire loyalty, new female employees from the branch offices, known as the "branch office girls", were brought to corporate headquarters for personal introductions. This program composed the bulk of female employee investment. The company also increased education requirements for male inspectors and managers; inspectors were to have completed some college and managers were expected to be college graduates.[13] The company preferred to hire women with college training, but did not enforce this policy. According to a 1926 manual, age, experience, previous employment history, and domestic conditions more importantly defined appropriate female employment traits:

> The stenographic work consists of taking dictation, editing letters, and copying reports. As a general rule, a girl 21 or 22 years old will produce the best results. Beginners can be from 18 to 20. Advanced stenographers should be from 20 to 24 years of age. She should be a high school graduate; a girl with some college training is desirable. There is nothing especially difficult about our work from an educational standpoint, but a stenographer must be able to spell and write correctly . . . . We would not care to employ a girl who has been working over five years, or one who has changed positions much. It is hard for them to adapt themselves to our organization. We should employ girls who live at home, and whose home surroundings and training have been desirable. Girls who are about the country working for a time in different cities are not permanent and should not be employed.[14]

Eventually, training programs expanded beyond inspectors and managers and allowed women to participate in company-sponsored employee educational classes. These correspondence courses taught women additional skills about their own jobs and those of others, providing a means for advancement. And women took advantage of the courses; in 1933, sixteen out of twenty participants were women.[15]

Despite such training, only college-educated men or former inspectors assumed management roles in the branch offices and later in the home office. Promotion to management positions for men required numerous transfers and travel. Women transferred within the home office and even occasionally to branch offices for short periods of time, but always in clerical capacities.

Susan Hecker is a good example of a long-term female employee who improved her skills and attempted to advance occupationally, but who was never identified in company literature as a professional. In 1934, Hecker celebrated fifteen years of service with the company and was appropriately acknowledged in the *Inspection News* with an article summarizing her career. Shortly after her ten-year anniversary, she began to write articles in the *Inspection News* on trends in insurance underwriting, a field that engaged few women. Although recognized as a specialist in fire insurance and the study of ethnic origins—a "polite" term for insurance coverage for Blacks—her position with the company was ambiguous; she was not an underwriter, nor simply a clerical worker. It is possible that she was such a unique hybrid that existing nomenclature failed to describe her work.[16] Her example, however, typifies the pattern of women's long-term work histories at Retail Credit Company.

IN THE OFFICE AND BEYOND

Management's attitude toward women at Retail Credit Company was a curious mix of paternalistic concern and hard-nosed efficiency. Policies encouraged women to perfect their business skills, but indirectly expressed the personal convictions of the company's founders that women possessed emotional frailties unsuitable for success in the business world. As noted, female employees could advance beyond low-level clerical work, but only into such positions as librarian, editor, and stenographic supervisor. Positions that extended women's authority only over other women or, indirectly, over male employees. Women, such as Susan Hecker, who never married, strove to break through the occupational ceiling established for female employees. Hecker possessed a competitive nature, which she exhibited in company sporting events where she won several tennis and golf titles. Despite her preparations, she never assumed a position of authority within the management hierarchy. So why did women like Susan Hecker stay on at Retail Credit Company?

Despite the constraints placed upon women's advancement at Retail Credit Company, pride in one's work and the company were significant factors in employee fealty. The company took great pride in the high quality of both its male and female employees. Not just any woman could work for the Retail Credit Company. The company clearly stated that women and men must come from good families, preferably local; women should live at home and their home surroundings and training should be desirable. The company acquired this information in rigorous pre-employment screening through personal history reports, which were similar to the credit-rating reports that inspectors compiled for credit or insurance applicants. Each report investigated school records, previous employment, family background, and personal standing in the community. The company closely examined prior employment and unemployment to assure that all the individual's time was accounted for.[17]

Association with the Retail Credit Company held considerable social value in the business world and evoked strong loyalties among many employees. Despite the invasive and controlling aspects of many company policies, employees regularly endorsed the company in the pages of the *Inspection News* and *The Roundtable*. They cited Cator Woolford's rigid code of personal and business integrity as a source of pride. Company executives emphasized through social gatherings and frequent articles in the house organs what they considered appropriate social and business interactions. Annually, the company sponsored a party to welcome new employees and celebrate the company's progress. Cator Woolford hosted these formal parties at his country estate, "Jacqueland," in Druid Hills, an elite residential section of Atlanta. The company invited all employees, dubbed the "Retail Credit Company Family," to attend; the guest list often totaled 250 employees. Posing for portraits with their new employees, the Woolfords and the executive officers clearly presented an image of gentility and generosity. Cator Woolford assumed the roles of father, patron, and superior social example through these well-publicized events. By contrast, annual branch office fetes were relaxed, often held at a nearby recreation area, and featured ball games, barbecue, and informal attire.

The atmosphere in the Atlanta home office mirrored the social philosophy of the company founders. As employers and owners, the Woolfords felt an obligation to provide examples for their employees; they accomplished this through familial, even paternalistic, rhetoric, imagery, and action. Company executives urged Retail Credit Company employees to envision their work place as a home and their co-workers as a family. Loyalty, like familial duty, was expected and frequently expressed by both employees and management. Bill Cordes, a branch office manager and home office executive, wrote to his former employer Walter C. Hill that "[m]y admiration, yes even love for Mr. Cator is something very personal and precious to me and considerable of it overflows to Mr. Guy, to you and Jim Malone and others in the builder group of our wonderful company."[18]Employees affectionately addressed the Woolfords as "Mr. Cator" and "Mr. Guy" and were encouraged to do so through the company publications. While management policies at times seemed stern and unyielding, many long-term employees apparently believed that these policies, which emanated from the executive's personal convictions, were equitable and laced with an abiding affection.

> It is just remarkable how the Retail Credit Company people hold the love and interest of everyone who has ever been associated with them. I have often tried to analyze the force that lies back of this feeling and, in retrospect, I think of what, in the Retail Credit Company, I remember best. You will not be surprised to know that I think most often of the justice which I saw prevailing in the organization. Difficulties came, as they will do, but I always sensed the fact that great effort was made for the best interest of each individual. And I think with a great deal of pleasure of the feeling I had that the whole company was behind me and I also felt my every effort was appreciated. That, in itself, is an inspiration.[19]

The company cultivated these personal bonds between employees and the Woolfords by publishing anecdotes about Mr. Cator's marriage, his personal and business travels, and the evolution of his family. As a prominent Atlanta businessman, Cator Woolford actively promoted civic improvement. Through personal wealth and an ethic of community service, Woolford established the Community Employment Service, a city-wide free placement agency; financed a vocational guidance program in Atlanta's public schools; and personally initiated a dental clinic in the city's schools.[20] While Cator Woolford actively presided over company operations as president, the house organs portrayed him as sage, philanthropic, affectionate, possessing unquestionable family and business loyalty, and most importantly, worthy of admiration from all employees.

Because Cator Woolford's life took on heroic proportions, his successors continued to operate in his shadow even after his retirement in 1932. At that time, Cator Woolford handed over the company reins to Guy and comfortably assumed the mantle of company founder. The Boston office sent its regards. "It was seconded and approved by the meeting that the Boston Office offer Mr. Woolford our felicitations and express our love and loyalty to him . . . ."[21] The remaining company officers, Guy Woolford, Walter C. Hill, James C. Malone, C. M. Frederick, and George A. Bland also adopted a resolution wishing Mr. Cator well.

Upon Cator Woolford's retirement, some immediate changes occurred in the tenor of personnel management. Cator Woolford resigned in what some historians consider the lowest point of the Depression. At the end of 1932, the company officers published the state of company operations. The new officers established a management and inspector incentive plan with cash rewards, limited mostly to managers. They also trimmed the service reward system of cash awards for long-term employees although they indicated that they intended to resume some type of long-service plan when the economic conditions improved. Salaries were cut by 4 percent for all employees. In addition, reduced business meant reduced personnel needs, but the "compulsion of civic leadership" deterred management from outright dismissals. Instead, men and women who left, especially women who married, were not replaced. "One girl was released," the report noted, "whose people were in well-to-do circumstances."

When Hopf and Company was consulted in 1933 to help identify personnel and operational problems between the home office and field workers, Hopf concluded that "[t]he company has reached a stage in development where it is no longer possible to permit solution of vitally important problems . . . to remain among the intermittent and passive concerns of all executives." In brief, personnel decisions needed to be placed in the hands of trained personnel managers operating in a centralized department. Hopf also stated that many operating problems stemmed from inspectors performing too many clerical tasks and recommended that clerical work receive full scrutiny "with the objects of cutting out all unnecessary steps and records, . . . standardizing the order of performance, and . . . compressing the time element into the smallest possible compass."[22] The company's future, the Hopf report concluded, lay in the quality of inspectors and management, and stated that all efforts should be made to improve and retain these valuable employees.

Hopf's recommendations encouraged less executive authority in personnel management of field inspectors and managers and more pragmatic use of centralized personnel authority. The report generally discouraged the use of standardization except to improve clerical work efficiency. Thus, male-dominated positions, such as field inspector and manager, would receive professional upgrades, while traditionally female clerical positions would be further routinized. At this point, company executives made a decision to abandon the familial and often paternalistic management practices of the company founders and institute bureaucratic authority over certain company functions, especially clerical work.

Throughout the 1910s and the 1920s, the Woolford brothers had operated the Retail Credit Company like a family business. While using scientific management to increase productivity among a growing staff, they imposed moral codes that created an exclusivity among the company's employees, and cultivated intense employee loyalty largely linked to a single personality, Cator Woolford. Employment at Retail Credit Company implied an acceptance and endorsement of certain social values that limited women's role in the business world. The feelings of Sara Baker likely typified many women's attitude at Retail Credit Company: "I am proud of my ten years' length of service, association with the Company has been enjoyable. I feel that it has done as much as any single factor in my life's development. It has provided me with a means of livelihood."[23] Baker did not applaud the opportunities available, or her success in the business world, but instead pointed to the economic function of work for a single woman.

Increasingly, single women found work a necessary and sometimes enjoyable aspect of their adult lives. Companies like Retail Credit Company employed hundreds of single women and created company policy to mold their workforce. This form of employee management mirrored the attitude of other social organizations in the city.

NOTES

1. *City Builder* V, no. 2 (April 1920): 9.

2. There are numerous scholarly works that address paternalism in the South. The most evocative portrayal of southern mill life is Jacqueline Dowd Hall, James Leloudis, Robert Korstad, Mary Murphy, Lu Ann Jones, and

Christopher B. Daly, *Like A Family: The Making of a Southern Cotton Mill World* (Chapel Hill: University of North Carolina Press, 1987). An early work, Melton A. McLaurin, *Paternalism and Protest: Southern Cotton Mill Workers and Organized Labor, 1875-1905* (Westport, Connecticut: Greenwood Publishing Corporation, 1971), while less comprehensive, places the origins of southern organized labor in context. Finally, David Carlton, *Mill and Town in South Carolina, 1880-1920* (Baton Rouge: Louisiana State University, 1982) traces the pervasive influence of mill policies in emerging towns and the divisive social attitudes created between mill operatives and town merchants, aided by political demagogues.

3. Sears Roebuck and Company established bonuses, anniversary checks, medical benefits, and employee organizations in the pre-World War I era, largely due to the efforts of one man, Elmer Scott. The employee organizations suffered the first cut-backs when Scott was transferred from Chicago to Dallas. Richard Sears did not approve of Scott's employee programs and expressed his delight that "all frills will be cut out. I know you want practice and not theory. Me too." Although Sears adopted employee medical benefits and profit sharing in 1912, in an attempt to humanize employer and employee relations, the company resisted establishing a centralized personnel department until 1925. The massive growth of its work force during the early 1920s required management to adopt systematic hiring, training, and promotional methods. Boris Emmet and John Jeuck, *Catalogues and Counters: A History of Sears, Roebuck and Company* (Chicago: University of Chicago Press, 1950), 276-292.

4. William A. Flinn, "History of Retail Credit Company: A Study in the Marketing of Information About Individuals" (Ph.D. dissertation, Ohio State University, 1959), 20.

5. The Home Office employed a total of 264 employees, 123 women in clerical positions in 1931 at the time of the Women's Bureau survey. Presumably, the company executives did not need manuals to perform their jobs. General interview, Retail Credit Company.

6. *Inspection News* and *Roundtable*, Equifax Library, Corporate Headquarters, Atlanta.

7. Retail Credit Company, "Report of Personnel Policies: Information Secured by Supervisors from Various Business Houses" June 1926, Equifax Library, Atlanta; Mr. Russell to Mr. Long, TL 28 March 1926; and Memo from Walter Hill to Cator Woolford, 20 April 1926, Correspondence, Equifax Library.

8. Personnel records were not available to the author so the occupational history of the company's female employees can only be surmised. I feel

confident that no women entered the male managerial ranks at the Retail Credit Company during the period 1912-1939.

9. Retail Credit Company, *Inspection News*, April 1932, 54; June 1932, 88; May 1934, 76; September 1934, 126; February 1934.

10. For a discussion of family labor systems and female clerical labor among Italian families in New York see, Miriam Judith Cohen, "From Workshop to Office: Italian Women and Family Strategies in New York City, 1900-1950" (Ph.D. diss., University of Michigan, 1978).

11. "A Seven Year Record in the Library" *Inspection News* 5 (November 1921): 83.

12. J. F. Forman, "Personnel Interest" *The Roundtable* 8 (September 1935): 36; George A. Bland "Pace-Setters of Business and Personal Conduct" *Inspection News* 20 (May 1935): 70.

13. Retail Credit Company, "Report of Personnel Policies: Information Secured by Supervisors from Various Business Houses" June 1926, TMs, Equifax Library, Atlanta.

14. Retail Credit Company, "Basic Policies and Practices and Instructions on Incidental Phases of the Personnel Investigation," 1926, TMs, Equifax Library, Atlanta.

15. *Roundtable* 6 (July 1933): 21.

16. "Fifteenth Anniversary," *Inspection News* 19 (March 1934): 40.

17. *Inspection News* 17 (June 1932): 83.

18. Bill Cordes, Attorney, to Mr. Walter C. Hill, TLS, 20 October 1959.

19. "Ave Retail Credit!" *Inspection News* 15 (March 1930): 36. Maybelle Jones Dewey, a former editor of *Inspection News*, wrote this letter of appreciation. She left the company to marry.

20. "Life of Cator Woolford", TMs, Equifax Library, Atlanta.

21. Retail Credit Company, Miscellaneous Correspondence, Boston Office Meeting Memo, 2 February 1932, Equifax Library, Atlanta.

22. Retail Credit Company, Hopf Report 1933-1934, Equifax Library, Atlanta.

23. Sara C. Baker, "Ten Years Completed" *Inspection News* 14 (May 1929): 79.

CHAPTER 4

Building Civic Bridges:
Building Business Consensus

Both Atlanta business men and women participated in civic activities that broadly aimed to improve the city's economy and fulfilled implied social responsibilities. The most prominent male civic group, the Atlanta Chamber of Commerce, supported an economic booster campaign, known as the Forward Atlanta Campaign, and expansion of municipal vocational education programs. Women's social and civic organizations, such as the Young Women's Christian Association (YWCA), the Atlanta Women's Club, the Atlanta Business and Professional Women's Organization (BPW), and the Women's Division of the Atlanta Chamber of Commerce, frequently organized through churches or ecumenical agencies or as members of homogenous socio-economic groups. As work became more common in women's lives, they also began to organize through shared professional or occupational associations. Participation in civic activities in the early twentieth century was routinely divided by gender. Women's clubs emerging in the 1920s and the 1930s began to blur these time-honored distinctions and significantly impacted women's public lives. Increasingly, women's book clubs and prayer circles in Atlanta participated in Chamber of Commerce activities and often went further and devised their own programs to advance women's occupational opportunities, enrich the city's cultural life, and enhance the stature of their gender.

Businessmen gained appreciably from the kind of civicism sponsored by the Chamber of Commerce. The Chamber believed that economic advancement promised occupational opportunities for all

Atlanta men and women and led to better cultural programs, regional recognition, and even moral superiority. Broadening specific municipal programs such as education, helped businessmen's personal commercial pursuits in addition to fulfilling civic guardianship.

The Atlanta businessman promoted educational programs and employment bureaus as a means to extend the city's occupational opportunities to its citizens. Through these efforts, businessmen directly affected the occupational paths of female white-collar workers. White collar, or business women included a broad range of women workers from retail clerks, to telephone operators, to clerical workers. These occupations varied considerably regarding required education or skills, working conditions, and wage or salary levels. Industrial work also employed a variety of women workers, from the cotton mill worker to women in commercial laundries and food processing.

Women's organizations, like the YWCA and the Women's Division of the Chamber of Commerce, also affected female white-collar workers. On the national level, the YWCA sponsored labor reform aimed primarily at industrial workers through legislation, negotiation, and direct assistance. White-collar workers received considerably less political attention from the YWCA than industrial workers, but the YWCA did seek to influence business girls in the city. Business women's programs focused on preparing young women for business careers through training. But more importantly, the YWCA aimed to protect business girls, many migrating to the city on their own, by sponsoring residences and business "girls" leagues. The YWCA's advocacy for business women revealed the organization's roots in the Progressive reform era and promoted the adoption of middle-class values by a broad class of working women. The Women's Division of the Chamber of Commerce, composed of professional and white-collar business women, avoided direct employment assistance or training but it championed women's participation in civic affairs. Despite these efforts, neither organization spearheaded efforts to transform the domestically oriented civic roles adopted or inherited by socially active women like themselves into politically potent civic roles that professional women increasingly sought.

THE CIVIC IDEAL

The Atlanta Chamber of Commerce defined civicism and businessmen's promotional efforts in 1916 as the "Atlanta Spirit." The

City Builder's editor Louie Newton coined the phrase to promote the personal qualities of the city's leading businessmen and to inspire Atlanta citizens with confidence in their leaders. Hoping to rally the populace toward common goals of economic and moral development, businessmen engaged in rhetorical filibusters on social responsibility and economic expansion. Often, they illustrated their philosophy through well understood religious analogy, combining urban patriotism and moral uplift. "To experience the 'Atlanta Spirit' was to undergo a veritable religious conversion, to engage in an act of faith." At other times, these booster campaigns were more direct, applying a heavy dose of urban propaganda. Organized boosterism reached a climax in Atlanta when the Chamber of Commerce launched its Forward Atlanta advertising blitz in 1926. The Chamber, composed of powerful and persuasive businessmen and political leaders, authoritatively molded the city's growth through private and public means to serve their interests. The Atlanta Spirit and its accompanying rhetoric softened criticism of self-interest aimed at businessmen and persuaded the community that economic growth and expansive civic interest formed the basis of social responsibility.[1]

Other southern cities launched parallel booster campaigns, and their leaders frequently shared common ideals, described alternately as boosterism, civic-mindedness, urban patriotism, and civicism. Through programs initiated and financed by a business and political alliance, such as publicly funded educational programs that vocationally trained workers, businessmen exercised their social responsibilities and profited commercially. For example, businessmen actively promoted employment placement services. In addition, many male civic organizations retooled their volunteer networks to encompass substantial civic activities established by women's organizations.

Between 1910 and 1920, southern business leaders grappled with ways to advance their cities but avoid the pitfalls experienced by rapid urbanization. Business leaders recognized that frequent annexations and divided interests caused chaotic city growth, which in turn threatened economic, political, and social control. Southern urban leaders urged adoption of comprehensive plans. Characterized by pragmatic functionalism, the city plans aimed to minimize the unstable boom and bust economies which vaulted small towns into big metropolises and radically altered social conditions. Civic leaders in Memphis, New Orleans, and Atlanta concentrated on consolidating economic and political gains in the region's mature cities. This philosophy differed greatly from the region's nineteenth-century civic pioneers' advancement of all growth, regardless of its chaotic nature. Ultimately, business leaders wanted to safeguard their investments through rigorous planning controls.[2]

Street transportation and zoning measures dominated the planning movement in the South. Atlanta planners devised zoning ordinances to disperse the population and formalize racial residential segregation. Initially, Atlanta real estate interests opposed municipal zoning fearing an infringement on their private property rights. Despite this opposition, an Atlanta zoning law passed the City Council in 1922 and formalized largely existing racial residential segregation. The passage coincided with increased Ku Klux Klan activity and culminated in the 1922 mayoral election of Walter Sims, an acknowledged Klansman.[3]

Concentrated efforts by southern municipal leaders on racial zoning segregation weakened other planning efforts and contradicted the community solidarity ideal associated with the Atlanta Spirit.[4] White civic leaders' efforts throughout the 1920s excluded meaningful black participation in city planning measures, and though rhetorically encouraging broad participation in economic regeneration, business leaders avoided truly populist civic and economic policies. "Clearly implied by all [civic and business leaders'] statements and policies was the proviso that the 'public interest' was best determined by persons like themselves."[5]

Atlanta business leaders, like others across the nation, formulated a doctrine of social responsibility and adopted a motto based in idealism and oriented toward community service. Self-regulation among business and civic organizations served as the keystone of social responsibility doctrines like the Atlanta Spirit. Repeatedly, the *City Builder* displayed advertisements and feature columns admonishing the "knocker" to join the civic cause. Manifest in a number of ways, businessmen's social responsibility encompassed participation in urban reform and increased worker welfare benefits. But as time passed, this service-mindedness often served a more active role as a business promotion than as a practical business application. Management recognized that better relations with employees, stockholders, customers, and the public produced as many economic benefits as ruthless capitalist enterprise. But as a group they did not necessarily embrace moral or social concerns.[6] In Atlanta, the civic service rhetoric quickly spread among the clergy, journalists and editors, public servants, and municipal politicians. Cornelius Ayer, the Chamber's membership chairman, warned the booster and the knocker alike that:

> the growling man is here and he is not a member of our Chamber of Commerce. What shall we do with him? . . . No man with an open mind can criticize the Chamber of Commerce idea. No sensible man can question the tremendous fact that cities grow faster and richer, when their business expansion and forethought for the future emanates from the Chamber of Commerce.[7]

Not all businessmen aspired to join the Chamber of Commerce. But few men with any hopes for civic recognition could avoid the financial and social leverage wielded by the Chamber. The Atlanta Chamber used its economic and social influence to discipline or exclude knocking individuals, barring membership in key social and civic organizations or withholding credit extensions.[8]

Clearly, the Chamber desired a united civic effort and utilized its considerable influence to shape the city's social, educational, and physical growth. Undoubtedly, the commercial-civic elite benefited both publicly and privately. Their civic efforts also affected Atlanta's less privileged citizens. Regardless of race, gender, or class the entire Atlanta community suffered, celebrated, or stagnated as a result of Atlanta's New South civicism.

During the 1920s, several programs sponsored by businessmen directly influenced the enlarging female white-collar workforce. Atlanta businessmen and educators created public high school commercial programs and promoted occupational training, using public funds, which prepared their future and existing personnel. Many of these workers would be women. Business and civic leaders also promoted efficient employment bureaus and rallied the support of women's organizations like the YWCA and the Women's Division of the Chamber of Commerce. Female civicism, established in women's social and religious organizations, cleared a seat for women on the Atlanta booster bandwagon.

Educational and employment placement programs for young white women entering the growing clerical workforce intended to advance Atlanta women's economic opportunities. Yet, openly acknowledging women's economic importance during the 1920s and 1930s was not common, even among women's organizations devoted to the business woman. Through influence and direct action, Atlanta businessmen divided civicism along gender lines when possible, allowing women to participate in civic activities much more broadly than before. However, businessmen also excluded working women or their advocates from participating in decisions that affected many women. Businessmen's influence in public education programs exemplifies how business leaders applied civicism to serve their best interests and what roles they allowed women's organizations to take.

EDUCATING THE OFFICE WORKFORCE

In 1869, the Atlanta City Council voted to establish a public school system. The white population, chagrinned by the presence of four missionary-sponsored schools for black children, urged the council to improve the educational opportunities for white children. In 1871, the Atlanta public school system operated nine white schools and four black schools, the latter formerly operated by missionaries. By 1873, the white educational system included five coeducational grammar schools and Boys High and Girls High. Black education in Atlanta's public schools proved inferior from its inception, and secondary schools for blacks languished until the establishment of Booker T. Washington High School on Atlanta's west side in 1924.[9]

Secondary education for white students flourished by comparison, although educational funds commonly failed to meet the system's needs. Throughout the 1880s and 1890s, increased enrollments strained the inadequate budgets of the Board of Education. But educators refused to inform the public that insufficient money meant poor education and inadequate school facilities. The resulting school environments often were unhealthy for students and teachers. Commonly built of wood, the buildings were susceptible to fire, poorly heated, and some unequipped with water closets or drinking water.[10]

Girls High School opened in 1872 to provide classical educations to Atlanta's young women. Despite resistance from Atlanta's elite toward public secondary education, more than half of the Girls High student body came from affluent families; few had working-class origins. The school served a minority of eligible school-age students and enrolled approximately 30 percent of the total elementary school enrollment.[11] By 1889, curriculum changes brought a more diversified and larger student enrollment to Girls High.

Pioneer educator, State Senator Hoke Smith, and commercial-civic leaders persuaded reluctant taxpayers to finance public secondary education. Within twenty years, the Board approved publicly funded business curricula.[12] On June 29, 1889, the Atlanta Board of Education officially adopted business courses at Girls High.

> We recommend that a business course, be introduced with the next session, to interfere in no way with the present literary course, but that diplomas be given in future for the Literary Course as now established, the diplomas to be entirely distinct and in no way dependent upon one another.
>
> While the practical studies which we will thus introduce next fall are few, we present them upon a plan which will allow additions in the future, and we hope that in a few years the business course in the Girls High School of Atlanta will embrace every line of study by the aid of which our girls can learn competent support.[13]

Business classes also brought changes to the socioeconomic makeup of the Girls High student body. Between 1896 and 1910, when a separate facility for commercial secondary education was established, nonelite student enrollments increased in the commercial secondary school by approximately 14 percent. Greater participation by nonelite students was evident in decreases among upper-class student enrollments, between 1881 and 1896, and increases among middle-class students.[14]

Proponents of publicly funded business training elicited support from the business community and appealed to the possibilities of female economic independence. Mrs. Corinne Hamilton Douglas, trained in law at the University of Illinois, became the first female principal of Girls High in 1888. Addressing the graduating normal class in 1889, Douglas directly appealed to businessmen for commercial education support.

> The public school is the place for [business training]. The public money is given to support the public school. . . . The study of shorthand, besides giving the girls means of independence serves as well as other subjects for mental training, thus accomplishing two of the highest objects of education. Next year we shall probably add typewriting and other subjects until we have a fine technological school for girls, from which they may go into the world with confidence and independence.[15]

Supported by the Board, Mrs. Douglas launched an experimental business class with four students in 1888. The next year the Board voted to add a two-year commercial training program to the regular curricula. The business course subjects focused on practical arithmetic, "embracing the methods used by accountants in the employ of bankers," insurance and others, rhetoric aimed at the improvement of letter writing skills, spelling, bookkeeping, typewriting, and stenography. "Not a moment was wasted on extras."[16] Superintendent William F. Slaton lauded the business program and claimed that "the popularity of this addition to this school is unprecedented and the pressure for its enlargement and expansion cannot long be ignored." Slaton felt that business course graduates proved their qualifications because the city's best offices employed them. "Many of the alumnae of the literary department," he further noted, "wisely take a complete course in the business department and are thus provided for an independent living, in case of misfortune." However, not all students supported the addition of business courses. Elizabeth McCallie, a self-proclaimed Atlanta business-girl, lamented that "the girls in the regular course regarded those taking business course as inferior to themselves."[17] Despite these unfavorable social implications, the program grew.

Businessmen supported educators' efforts to establish business curricula in public schools and encouraged young women to enroll. The increasingly popular business programs expanded female secondary education choices but also effectively channeled young women into low-level clerical occupations. Commercial training for women, both in the high schools and private business schools, meant preparation for clerical work, which required no further education. By contrast, commercial education at Boys High, not established until 1903, was not considered a terminal program. Businessmen applauded Atlanta's university commercial programs and encouraged young men to pursue business careers armed with collegiate training.[18] The lack of advanced commercial training for women implied that the rudimentary skills taught in the high schools or at the numerous private commercial "colleges" throughout the city was enough for business-minded women.

Private business training for young women consisted of short-term programs aimed at teaching the fundamentals of office work. Despite available public business training, private commercial schools flourished. Unlike public programs, private schools provided purely technical training, often completed in less than six months, which filled the lowest rungs in office hierarchies, usually typing and stenography positions.[19] The Crichton Business College, established in 1885, encouraged multiple skills among its graduates, but focused on the mechanical. "Professional and businessmen," the school brochure announced, "in employing bookkeepers and assistants almost invariably prefer those who can write shorthand and operate the typewriter." In 1925, the school boasted that both high school graduates and collegiate students now enrolled.[20] Many Girls High graduates supplemented their secondary schooling by attending private commercial schools. In 1922, approximately 14 percent received business training after graduation. Graduates of the 1936-1939 classes acknowledged pursing commercial courses at Crichton, Draughon's School of Commerce, and Marsh Business School before entering the business world. Educational requirements varied among Atlanta business concerns, but by the 1930s, companies universally required a high school degree and assumed that most women has pursued some business training.[21] Young females migrating to Atlanta from the rural South could work odd jobs while completing a private business course and enter the clerical ranks where most women entered them, at the bottom.

Crowding at Girls High, where enrollments increased from 657 in 1900 to 807 in 1910, precipitated the establishment of English-Commercial High. In 1909, Boys High had established Technological High, separating the vocational students from the literary students. Girls High followed suit in 1911 and transferred 154 female commercial students to the deanery of St. Phillips Church to pursue business curriculum, establishing English-Commercial High.[22] Annie T. Wise led these commercial students. Unlike Technological High, which remained all-male until after World War II, the all-female English-Commercial High merged with the business department of Boys High to create the first coeducational secondary school, renamed Commercial High.

Commercial High reflected several attempts by Superintendent Robert Guinn and others to consolidate and democratize Atlanta's secondary schools. Guinn felt that many students completing grammar school could not attend high school; their families needed the income they could provide and the secondary school curriculum reflected elitist educational goals. Guinn did not stand alone in his opinions. In 1914, the Board engaged Celeste Parrish, State Supervisor for the Department of Education, to survey the school system. Parrish faulted Atlanta high schools' limited curriculum. In particular, she reported that Girls High did not prepare its students for goals outside of college or office work. "At least fifty percent of Atlanta girls will need to work for a living. For this you are offering them training in office work alone." Parrish recommended adding home science, child training, and vocational work to provide options for the majority who would not attend college. Parrish specified merging Girls High and English-Commercial High and establishing a university system with elective courses to break the vocational gap. The Board only acted upon the recommendation to provide domestic training.[23]

Business training, eliminated from Girls High with the establishment of English-Commercial High in 1911, did not return until 1923. The removal of business students from Girls High again altered the class composition of the school, generally reducing the number of lower-class students. Middle-class and upper-class students continued to pursue literary programs and many were attracted to further education in the normal school program. However, by 1921, the Girls High bank, established to give high school girls practical personal financial experience, served as an entering wedge for business courses. The school added Bookkeeping and Business English in 1923, followed by filing courses in 1928, and finally shorthand courses in 1934. Girls High's principal described the reinstated business courses as an "important inclusion in a cosmopolitan school."[24]

Nationally, publicly funded commercial education emerged in the post-World War I period. This growth stemmed from widespread economic prosperity and the increasingly popular notion of civic efficiency, both closely associated with a prosperous business culture.[25] Superintendent William F. Slaton, serving from 1879 to 1907, ardently supported publicly funded business education. His predecessors, Robert Guinn and William Dykes, disputed consolidation efforts, but did not challenge business hegemony in education. Municipal public school reform by business interests both enhanced the city's image and molded a productive workforce capable of enlarging Atlanta's commercial capacity.

Two events occurred in the early 1920s that illustrate well the pervasive business influence in Atlanta's public education. In 1921, the Atlanta Opportunity School, authorized by the Smith-Hughes Act of 1917, extended vocational education to those unable to attend public high schools. In 1923, junior high schools were introduced, which significantly extended existing vocational training programs. Both education initiatives reflected attempts to provide practical post-elementary schooling to students unable to attend secondary schools. Night schools also operated for working men and women and focused on commercial courses. Female night schools experienced some travails, at first lacking sufficient enrollments. However, by 1910, with the support of the Woman's Exchange, the girls' night school program was reinstated. In 1916, white night schools combined under Central Night School and served concurrently with other vocational programs.[26]

Vocational and occupational training were terms used interchangeably among education advocates and civic leaders in the early twentieth century. Although many vocational programs leaned heavily toward teaching manual skills for trades or factory work, they also included corporate training, such as commercial or business courses, and "life" skills, particularly domestic science, child training, and home economics. By the 1920s, vocational training encompassed most skills required to participate in an industrial and urbanized society, in which mechanization defined many jobs. Vocational training institutes imparted some generalized skills to workers, but also sought to teach future personnel "respect for the imperatives of the corporate form of employment."[27] Within vocational education programs, clerical, also called commercial or business, training gained prestige, due to its white-collar association. However, scientific management techniques and an increased reliance on machines diminished the cerebral quality of white-collar work. As vocational programs expanded, commercial training incorporated more manual skills than analytical ones.[28]

The Opportunity School, enthusiastically supported by Atlanta businessmen, benefited commercial concerns directly through part-time work and study programs. The junior high schools resulted from a School Board initiative to encourage students to remain in school beyond the elementary years and served to counsel future high school enrollers toward suitable continued education. In effect, both schools trained and vocationally counseled a generation of laborers and clerks.

The Smith-Hughes Act provided matching funds to states and municipalities for vocational education programs. Opportunity schools appeared in numerous cities responding to the Act's mandate to provide meaningful vocational education.[29] The Atlanta Opportunity School offered vocational courses to persons over fourteen years of age and included:

> Besides the regular grammar school studies, there are classes in salesmanship, merchandising, advertising, typing, stenography, filing, bookkeeping, secretarial work, business English, rapid calculation, commercial law, mechanical drawing, office practice, study of vocations, Americanization, English literature, dressmaking, home sewing for business girls, beauty parlor work, cooking and home making, millinery, auto mechanics, etc.[30]

The Opportunity School held classes in the Commercial High School Annex and described its program as a continuation of grammar school work. The emphasis, though, leaned heavily toward commercial courses and mechanical training for office work. Approximately 60 percent of the students worked day jobs and attended classes a few hours each week. The remaining 40 percent actively pursued commercial training, but did not work. In 1921, another study commissioned by the Board of Education, described the Opportunity School objective.

> This school is attempting to supply the worker's lack of previous experience and to raise the academic standards of both young and old people engaged in commercial fields. The rapid growth of this school is sufficient evidence that there is a dire need of short intensive unit courses for those who have not the time or previous training to spend four years in the Commercial High School.[31]

The school began with one teacher and twelve students in February, 1921. By June, the school had expanded to two teachers with 102 students. Five departments offered vocational guidance and placement, general continuation courses, commercial trades, and extension work. The student body consisted, chiefly, of employees of 135 Atlanta business firms. Seventy-five saleswomen, fifty-nine salesmen, and fifty-eight general clerical workers enrolled the first year. Yet, the 1927 "Rules and Regulations" of the Board of Education rejected claims that the school served as a business preparatory school.

> No student shall be enrolled in the commercial classes, such as stenography and bookkeeping, unless he is employed or, if temporarily out of employment, has studied them previously; that is the commercial classes of the Opportunity School shall not be used as

a preparatory business college, but as part-time and continuation courses.[32]

By 1932, the Opportunity School curriculum operated under only three departments: Part-Time General Continuation Department, the Commercial Department, and the Trades Department, maintaining an average annual enrollment of 1,000 students. Clearly viewed as a progressive undertaking, the Opportunity School enjoyed widespread support. Advocates praised the vocational agenda which opened doors for wage earners, "especially youthful wage earners in the city of Atlanta."[33]

Young women benefited greatly from the Opportunity School, as affirmed by large female attendance (See Table 4.1 below). Between 1932 and 1938, female enrollment, especially among unemployed women greatly exceeded male attendance.

Enrollments increased from several hundred to several thousand between 1921 and 1938, but students continually failed to attend the school regularly enough to complete graduation certificates. Spotty attendance vexed school administrators, but they felt that limited training served better than none at all. Employers must have agreed. Cooperative part-time classes were arranged to accommodate both employers and students, and curricula often catered to the needs of individual firms. For example, eight courses added in 1932-33 taught show card lettering to a group of Western Union employees. Retail shops benefited from extension salesmanship courses attended by Davison-Paxon, M. Rich, J. M. High, F. W. Woolworth, and S. H. Kress store employees among others.[34]

The Opportunity School afforded clerical training through Secretarial and Bookkeeping classes available in 1921, followed by Calculator or Comptometer classes in 1929, General Clerical in 1935, and Steno-Comptometer classes in 1937. To earn a completion certificate the school required students to attend nine to eighteen months of schooling. At first, few students garnered certificates. However, between 1928 and 1938 graduation rates increased steadily in all clerical courses. Equally popular Trade Millinery and Beauty Culture courses also experienced rising completion rates. School officials attempted to ensure the success of clerical courses through vocational counseling. "It is believed, . . . that this curriculum will become quite useful," school administrators argued, "as many students

Table 4.1: Enrollment of the Opportunity School, 1932-1937 Employed, Partially Employed, and Unemployed

Year	Number				Employed				Partial Emplt				Unemployed				Total
	M	%	F	%	M	%	F	%	M	%	F	%	M	%	F	%	
1932	464	22	1611	78	196	42	492	31	145	31	413	26	123	26	706	44	2075
1933	797	29	1956	71	534	67	640	33	85	11	267	14	178	22	1049	54	2753
1934	582	23	1962	77	348	60	515	26	51	11	142	8	183	31	1305	67	2544
1935	479	17	2392	83	231	48	723	30	66	14	159	6	182	38	1510	63	2871
1936	460	17	2254	83	282	61	528	23	53	12	357	16	125	27	1369	61	2714
1937	880	29	2174	71	662	75	695	32	47	5	356	16	171	19	1123	52	3054

Source: Myrtle B. Durham, "History of the Atlanta Opportunity School," Table V, 70.

who probably would never be employable as secretaries or stenographers are being guided by the faculty into the general clerical curriculum."[35]

Attempts to abolish the school occurred twice, in 1924 and 1932. Both attempts stemmed from the Board's inadequate budget, although one appeal came from Mr. L. W. Arnold, President of Southern Shorthand and Business School. Some Board members felt regular public schools suffered because the Opportunity School diverted needed funds. Arnold claimed that the Opportunity School unfairly competed against private business schools which received no public funding. The School Board, supported by the business community, the Atlanta *Constitution*, and Superintendent Willis A. Sutton, defeated both attempts to abolish the school.[36] Criticism by contemporaries and later scholars alike faulted the business community for serving their own interests through publicly funded education. The regular school system suffered financially and little real effort by the business community to support needed education bonds materialized. Instead, "pet projects" like the Opportunity School received public funding and businessmen's sanction. For example, in 1928, the Opportunity School was relocated to larger quarters, yet the Normal Training School, the principal source for trained teachers, closed.[37] Despite the unqualified need for trained teachers, the School Board failed to provide adequate professional training. By contrast, the Atlanta business community strengthened its labor supply by its strenuous support of the Opportunity School.

Willis Sutton served as Superintendent of Atlanta's city schools from 1921 to 1944. Although his relationship with the city's business interests was often troubled, it did not significantly affect the growth of vocational education. Commercial High School and the Opportunity School expanded under his leadership. Sutton attempted to reassure businessmen that vocational and cultural educational curricula could coexist without the schools succumbing entirely to scientific management techniques. Continually, Sutton emphasized the importance of cultural education and rebuffed repeated attempts to streamline music, language, and arts curricula for temporary fiscal solvency.[38]

Sutton avoided direct criticism of vocational curricula, but his arguments for cultural education won few converts among business leaders. Opponents on the Board and in the business community labeled Sutton's progressive education measures "frills" and repeatedly tried to eliminate them. Teachers supported Sutton's educational agenda and helped maintain curriculum consistency in elementary and junior high schools. But the senior high schools focused on college preparatory and practical training and failed to provide a continuum between the lower schools' cultural curricula and high school course work.[39] After serving twenty years as Superintendent, Sutton addressed the National Education Association in 1941. His essay, "Business and Education," implored business leaders to view educational programs more broadly.

> The one barometer of good business is the educational level, the culture level:. . . What did we do when the depression hit us? We said that the children could stop music. We said that Chautauqua would have to cease. . . . We said that the buying of books would have to end. We said the painting of pictures and the writing of poetry would have to cease . . . . maybe not last but first we said, "This question of the spirit of a teacher, it can live on half of what we have been paying it, and the schools can live on less."[40]

Despite his conflicts with the Board, Sutton did not forego the language of efficiency in his appeals to business interests. He argued that the programs of economy followed by the Board decreased the efficiency of the schools from 100 percent in 1926 to 66 percent in 1929.[41] The superintendent aimed to prove to businessmen that cultural education sharpened business acumen and pointed to the educated consumer. Third graders or fifth graders could not make intelligent choices in the marketplace, Sutton argued, whether they purchased food, clothing, or an insurance policy. To reassure businessmen, Sutton did not attempt to supplant vocational training with cultural programs.[42]

Dr. Sutton continually urged civic leaders to consider diversified education as a training tool for productive community members and future company employees. The Superintendent appealed to businessmen's practicality and their sense of social responsibility. However, not all business leaders felt the urgency to invest in long term educational programs when called upon to relieve community problems, especially employment concerns.

CIVIC RESPONSIBILITY AND THE COMMUNITY EMPLOYMENT SERVICE

The Community Employment Service, conceived by Cator Woolford, President of the Retail Credit Company, served Atlanta men and women seeking vocational guidance, permanent employment, or possibilities for promotion. The Service represented the consolidated efforts of businessmen, the Chamber of Commerce, and women's organizations to serve the unemployed. No profit was gained by the Service, and in many ways it embodied the Atlanta Spirit ideal more thoroughly than other business-sponsored civic efforts.

Employment services that appealed to clerical workers began in women's organizations. The Atlanta Young Women's Christian Association (YWCA), established in 1901, added an employment listing and placement service to its business girls boarding home in April 1905. That first month, the YWCA recorded sixteen positions secured for women seeking employment. It is not clear whether YWCA membership was required in order for women to utilize the service. The Women's Exchange, which operated a fee-based employment bureau and sold rural women's handicrafts, shared quarters with the YWCA in the downtown business district. The YWCA agreed to allow the Exchange to use the YWCA name in its advertisements in exchange for paying the YWCA a 50 cent fee and a portion of every placement fee received. The YWCA did not charge for its placement service. In 1907, Atlanta women seeking employment placement had at least two choices. By 1908, the YWCA had absorbed the operations of the Women's Exchange.[43]

The Atlanta Chamber of Commerce approached Cator Woolford in 1915 to investigate initiating a placement program for Atlanta's unemployed. Woolford owned the Retail Credit Company, an Atlanta-based credit rating concern with numerous branch offices. No city-sponsored programs existed, and the unemployed relied on private charity organizations for work relief or placement. Woolford recommended establishing an agency removed from charity that applied "sound business methods." He also agreed to finance the operation, initially. The new organization, called the Clearing House for Unemployment, established offices in the Chamber of Commerce Building and served unemployed men and women in all occupations.[44]

The Clearing House promoted the scientific application of personnel management. In 1916, the Clearing House added a vocational guidance counselor to give "guidance and training to local high school graduates and to men and women who were misfits in their jobs or who desired to work for promotion." Joseph P. McGrath, Chairman of the employment service in 1923, summarized the misfit employee as "the kind of help that . . . float[s] around promiscuously" and disrupts loyal employees. In 1917, Woolford also founded the Atlanta Personnel Association composed of various city business representatives. The Association directed its efforts toward impressing businessmen with the responsibility for absorbing Atlanta's public school graduates. The Association also directly aided students through job placement. Woolford felt that vocational counseling in the public schools would answer student's employment questions and avoid later personnel problems. Taking the initiative, Woolford established the School Employment Service (SES) in 1921 with the cooperation of the Junior Division of the U.S. Employment Service. The SES served to promote hiring of graduating students of the regular high schools, the night schools, and the Opportunity School. Superintendent Sutton promoted the SES for graduates and dropouts alike. Proponents described the SES as the "sales department" of the public schools, marketing its graduates among Atlanta's business firms.[45]

The YWCA continued to operate its own employment bureau, even though the city maintained a similar program. Both the boarding home and the employment bureau noted an increase in the number of female transients seeking work during 1917 and 1918. In response to the great demand for employment services, the National Board authorized a salaried position to operate the overburdened Atlanta employment bureau. As Employment Secretary, Mrs. Scott filed the first detailed records on employment placement and boarding home residents and illustrated that clerical work positions were both highly sought and slightly more abundant than industrial employment. Secretary Scott recorded in June 1918 that forty-seven female industrial positions were sought and fourteen were filled. Sixty-six female applicants sought clerical positions and twenty-one were placed. In September, another twenty-nine female industrial workers applied and eighteen found work. Fifty-two prospective clerical workers registered and twenty were placed. For the two years the YWCA kept records (1917-1919), female clerical workers seeking employment had a lower placement ratio than industrial workers, but more women sought clerical positions

Table 4.2: YWCA Employment Bureau Placement 1919

Positions	Clerical	Industrial	Total
Sought	273	166	439
Percent	100	100	100
Placed	198	124	322
Percent	73	75	73

(see Table 2.2.). The YWCA consistently placed nearly three-quarters of the women seeking clerical (73 percent) and industrial work (75 percent). Industrial positions fared well, but fewer women sought them.

The YWCA stopped maintaining detailed records, indicating clerical and industrial positions sought and placed, by 1920. However, the number of women it served continued to increase until 1921. At that point, women again flooded the YWCA's Employment Bureau coming primarily from rural areas where an agricultural recession, resulting from depressed post-war cotton prices, significantly undermined small town employment opportunities. In February 1921, 359 women sought work in Atlanta through the YWCA, but only forty-six were placed (13 percent). In September, the Employment Bureau felt encouraged by the rising price of cotton and stated optimistically that increased female work opportunities would follow. By January 1922, the employment situation appeared to improve.[46]

The following year the Chamber of Commerce introduced a new program to alleviate the unemployment resulting from the regional cotton market depression. Continuing under the leadership of Cator Woolford, the Community Employment Service requested that the two employment agencies operated by the School Employment Service and the YWCA consolidate under the Community Chest and re-form as the Cooperative Employment Service (CES). Woolford and the Community Chest felt the three agencies replicated services and would operate more efficiently under one organization. The Community Chest approached the YWCA to consolidate all its eleemosynary operations under the Chest to facilitate city-wide charity efforts. Reluctantly, the YWCA surrendered its active Employment Bureau under the condition that it retain some financial authority concerning other YWCA fundraising efforts, particularly its residential building fund campaigns. The Chest agreed under one condition, that the YWCA postpone its fundraising efforts until the Chest completed its own.[47]

Counseled by Atlanta businessmen, the city's three free employment agencies combined their efforts and the Chamber of Commerce vigorously applauded their efforts, "now one splendidly equipped, efficiently conducted organization functions for the convenience of employers and the proper and free placement of the unemployed."[48] By 1926, the Chest requested that the YWCA transfer part of its Employment Service budget to the CES. After much discussion, the YWCA agreed to release the amount required to employ the employment service administrator and combine its independent services with the CES.[49]

Under the CES, Atlanta men and women gained a centralized employment bureau, but lost the efficiency characteristic of the YWCA program. Also, the combination of male and female employment services reduced the YWCA's significant contribution to women's occupational futures. A 1927 Chamber report on the success of the CES instead underlined its failure, relative to the YWCA's previous efforts. The CES boasted that it placed 6,749 applicants, which represented 36 percent of the needy in 1926. In earlier years, the YWCA placed an average of 73 to 75 percent of its applicants. By August 1927, the CES had placed only 138 women in office positions in three months, compared to the 198 women placed by the YWCA between March and September 1919.[50]

The CES's employment placement ratio improved as time went by, but the Community Chest proved inadequate as the city's sole charitable organization as the Depression approached. The CES increased its placement percentage by 1939, finding work for 58 percent of the applicants registered with the agency. The issue of gender-related self-help, however, stagnated within the CES. Atlanta's women's organizations had surrendered a significant means of helping their own.

"BOOSTING WITHOUT BOASTING": THE CONFINES OF WOMEN'S CIVICISM

Female civicism emerged in southern missionary societies and other church-related organizations in the 1880s and applied women's energies toward mitigating urban ills most often associated with poverty. Anne Firor Scott postulates that southern men considered women's public activity through missionary work nonthreatening even though women spoke for themselves, kept records, organized, and cultivated a social, even worldly consciousness, through their religious work. By 1900, southern women's organizational activities extended beyond Christian fellowship and proselytizing. These women organized libraries and settlement houses, expanded school programs, fought for the abolition of child labor, supported sanitation laws and the establishment of juvenile courts, and funded scholarships to send girls to college.[51] Darlene Roth advises scholars to view women's organizing activities within a cultural context and not restrict the significance of women's activism to a feminist or political construct. The club women Roth studied "were outwardly subordinate and yet created systems for themselves which were aggressive and consciously self-gratifying."[52]

Several Atlanta women's organizations emerged in the 1920s following the lead of late nineteenth-century clubs like the United Daughters of the Confederacy, the Daughters of the American Revolution, and the Colonial Dames examined by Roth. These earlier organizations, with elite female memberships, influenced their communities and other women by "confer[ring] social status and distinctions upon their members . . . and perpetuat[ing] value systems through the institutionalization of their corporate bodies." The elite women's clubs, although not politically potent, exercised great authority among adult women through their activities and the physical landmarks they created. "The underlying beat of their organizational march is duty, duty, duty . . . to women, to their home and family, to her community, her state and her country, to her race, and to her God."[53]

Typically, southern women's organizations progressed from missionary societies, to temperance societies, and finally, to secular women's clubs. Women who organized through churches promoted the observance of Christian values. The Women's Christian Temperance Union (WCTU) and the Young Women's Christian Association (YWCA) are notable examples. These organizations sprang from the earliest southern church societies. Speaking in New Orleans in 1882, Frances Willard introduced the WCTU to the South. The Union focused on the eradication of alcohol and by inference, sought to reform southern men and the coarser side of southern life.[54] The YWCA established a branch in Atlanta in 1901. From the beginning, YWCA Board members desired that in addition to providing assistance to the needy that a great emphasis be placed on the Association's spiritual features.

The Atlanta YWCA promoted social reform through progressive support programs administered by using Christian theology and concepts of self-discipline. The first annual meeting in 1903 recorded that the Atlanta women had established a gymnasium, a lunch room for women working downtown, and a circulating library. Bible classes and Sunday afternoon gospel meetings confirmed the YWCA's desire for spiritual, as well as physical, enrichment. Within the year, approximately 400 women and girls enjoyed the gymnasium and enrolled as members. The following year, the YWCA established a boarding home and greatly expanded its reputation as the most reliable source of aid for Atlanta's working women.[55]

Other Atlanta women's organizations shared these goals, many preceding the YWCA. A settlement house at the Fulton Bag and Cotton Mill established in 1902 by the Methodist Episcopal Atlanta Women's Board of City Missions initially provided white workers with medical and educational benefits. By 1920, the settlement furnished a night school, kindergarten, and day nursery. The Wesley Settlement House, established in 1895, provided similar services to young black girls. In July 1908, Lugenia Burns Hope created the Neighborhood Union to supply much needed social services to neglected black communities. The Gate City Free Kindergarten Association, organized by Hope in 1900, aided working mothers in the black community and established a strong link between social service and working women.[56]

The YWCA and the WTCU, as well as other female social welfare agencies continued their reform work throughout World War I and into the 1920s. As a result of community service performed by women during World War I, women's clubs emerging in the 1920s embraced activities characterized by cultural and moral objectives, but that also indicated political activism and economic awareness.

Fledgling Atlanta business women early heeded the call to civic duty from Mayor Asa Candler. On May 26, 1917, Adjutant General Van Holt Nash and Mayor Candler entreated Atlanta women to volunteer their clerical services toward national and civic duty. The mayor enrolled the women, not as individuals, but as National League for Women's Service members. Established January 27, 1917, the League enlisted women eager to contribute their share toward the world war. The League served primarily as a training association, encouraging women to perform men's work. Classes in stenography and typing graduated over one hundred women by August 1917. "The class was made up principally of women who had never felt the need of a business training, but when the necessity arose were ready to do their 'bit'." Public school teachers volunteered to teach the women much-needed clerical skills. "Much to the surprise of dubious friends, the interest in the women has never fagged and instead of closing with a mere handful of students" a second class enrolled an additional fifty women unable to enter the first course. The call to civic duty prevailed among these women even though the work they performed fell below their patriotic expectations. "No doubt the Mayor thought for us, it would be a pleasant recreation," a volunteer recalled, "but to those who stuck to the task from the beginning to the end, know what arduous labor was expended."[57]

By 1919, the Business Women's Suffrage Club, made up of leading business and professional women, rallied to the mayor's duty call. The club organized to broaden the prevailing definition of female civicism, and its goals included the enfranchisement of women, furthering women's education on civic and government affairs, and promoting the welfare of Atlanta and Georgia. "The club will endeavor to deepen in the individual woman a feeling of personal responsibility to other women whereby women of all classes may more directly work towards their own advancement and the bettering of conditions under which they live."[58] In this club, civic responsibility among women reached beyond selfless municipal service and provided benefits to their gender while promoting the city's welfare.

The Atlanta YWCA focused many social services and recreational programs upon needy women. The YWCA established noon meetings at the Nunnally Pants Factory and the Elsas-May Mills and encouraged women to attend educational programs. The Association also initiated prayer meetings at downtown department stores aimed at white-collar workers. At the urging of the National Board, the Atlanta YWCA sharpened its unfocused social welfare activities to help female industrial workers and department store clerks. These efforts remained paramount to the YWCA throughout the 1920s and 1930s. However, through the Boarding Home, educational classes, and an Employment Bureau, the Atlanta YWCA broadened its contact with the city's clerical workforce. In 1917, the National Board helped finance an Employment Bureau and sent a seasoned administrator to Atlanta. This agency helped hundreds of clerical workers find positions. By 1920, two National Secretaries arrived in Atlanta to conduct a survey of living and working conditions among the city's female clerical workforce.

These events marked a turning point in the efforts of the Atlanta YWCA.[59]

The National YWCA redirected its focus, between 1904 and World War I, from providing temporary aid to young working women to scrutinizing the social consequences of industrial capitalism and demanding social and economic reforms. The broad national directive urged regional YWCAs to hire staff members trained in social sciences, appoint industrial secretaries, and assist industrial working women by raising questions about working conditions.[60] In Atlanta, the YWCA encouraged industrial women workers to participate in their organization through lunch programs, Bible study classes, and educational activities. The association boasted that their extension work reached women in seven Atlanta factories.

The YWCA's work among industrial women dominated the rhetoric of the association and appeared remarkably progressive. However, the relationship between the organization and industrial women workers more closely resembled a parent-child relationship, with the YWCA promoting its benevolent authority, than an equal partnership based on mutual reform goals.

The YWCA activities with young white-collar workers, although serving a considerable number of young women, never garnered the attention afforded the Ys industrial reform activities. The business girls clubs met in the boarding home and created their own drama clubs, literary and prayer circles, and encouraged the formation of similar clubs both within and outside of the YWCA.[61] Two business clubs within the YWCA, the S.I.S.P. and the Clover Club, reflected an increasingly popular trend among business girls to enjoy the physical and social programs sponsored by the YWCA and to participate in the service goals of the association. The Spiritual, Intellectual, Social and Physical Club (SISP), organized in 1904 with fifty charter members, began as a gymnasium club among white-collar working girls. By 1905, a second business club, the Clover Club, organized and indicated the business girls' growing interests in current events, art, dancing, and community service, in addition to physical activity. Outwardly novel and progressive, the business girls clubs never attempted to engage in labor-related discussions or organizing activities. Instead, these clubs adopted the middle-class social and reformist goals common among the city's most prominent women's secular and religious organizations.

The industrial and business club programs illustrate conflicting attitudes present in organizations like the YWCA and among the girls themselves. By the 1920s, the YWCA's interaction with the two working women's groups strongly indicate the organization's perception of class status and its dependence on the business-civic elite. The YWCA's industrial programs adopted the principles of labor organization and education advocated by the national association, but little labor organizing or reform occurred in the city likely because the YWCA relied on the Community Chest and thus, city business leaders, for some of its funding. The YWCA business-girls clubs rarely focused on nonjob-related skills training and did not organize around labor-related principals, but mimicked middle-class women's organizations in their own clubs. Lisa Fine argues that the YWCA in Chicago promoted the conventionalization of clerical employment. The YWCA clubs and residences, by creating strong associations between middle-class values and clerical work, masked a significant labor and social movement as ordinary middle-class women's work even though national women's labor leaders had begun to recognize the fallacy of this assumption.[62]

Women's organizations during the 1920s, through national federation efforts, broadened their memberships and included working women; some created distinct organizations devoted to the urban business and professional woman. Typically, the new clubs were led by women who either did not work or engaged in professional pursuits. The clubs' rank and file members consisted predominantly of clerical workers and teachers.[63] The Atlanta Chamber of Commerce Business Women's Division organized with the intent to provide a forum for business women interested in civic activism. The Division prided itself on combining urban patriotism, domesticity, and idealism into effective feminine civicism. Its initial cultural development programs broadened over fifteen years to include social services and a heightened female agenda.

The organization began in 1921 as the Department of Women's Affairs within the Chamber of Commerce and described its mission, in a monthly *City Builder* column, as service oriented, not self-help. By 1922, the group changed its name to the Business Women's Division, but cautioned against extending services simply to business women. Miss Jessie Muse, principal of Girls High School and Chairman of the Division's Education Bureau, advised against conducting business courses. Other opportunities for commercial training were available throughout the city, she stated, citing the Opportunity School.[64]

In 1923, the Governing Board of the Business Women's Division included twelve "business women" all working in various occupations.

Susie Wailes sat on the Board and also worked as a secretary for the Scottish Rite bodies in Atlanta. Wailes, later to serve as president of the women's chamber organization, summarized the goals of the Business Women's Division. She emphasized the important, but subtle, role women needed to play in city building.

> There are values that such [commercial] development never can touch, the things that beautify and uplift, the aesthetic side of people, music, art, parks, playgrounds, cleanliness, hospitality, things that are expressive of a city's cultural life, can best be promoted by the women of the city, and it is to promote and develop these in keeping with the phenomenal commercial and industrial growth of Atlanta that we invite every woman interested in our city's welfare to join the Women's division.[65]

With this agenda, the Business Women's Division strove to enlarge its membership and enhance the cultural opportunities available to Atlanta's citizens. Two programs dominated the early activities of these female city builders. In 1925, the Division participated in a city-wide Clean-Up Campaign sponsored, in part, by the senior Chamber of Commerce. Within three years, the senior Chamber relinquished all its duties related to city beautification campaigns to the Division. The women began their program modestly by advocating and securing trash receptacles for the city streets. The 1928 "Our Town Clean Up and Beauty Campaign" committee, spearheaded by the Women's Club of Atlanta, asked the Division to enroll housewives in a nationwide urban effort called "Clean-Up and Paint-Up Campaign." The Division urged Atlanta women to put their instinctive housekeeping skills to work noting that women naturally carried the burden of their families' health and happiness. Housework drudgery, explained the Division, was shared by all women and this solidarity lessened the chore; that, and the prospect of building a beautiful city should inspire Atlanta women to participate.[66]

The Division, which dropped the "business" nomenclature in 1925, also sponsored National Music Week festivities. The music program fulfilled one of the Division's mandates, to culturally enrich the life of Atlanta's citizens. As it did in the beautification campaigns, the Division took its role in music appreciation seriously, noting, "it is fitting that the Woman's Division . . . should consecrate much of its time and energy to development along these lines."[67] Every year, the opera tours, local music talent, and church-sponsored recitals busied the organization's members for several months. The Division also added Better Homes Week, Better Dance, and an annual Artists' Recital to their cultural agenda.

In the next few years, the Women's Division gradually broadened its civic activities to include business women's political and economic interests. The Division also attempted to enlarge its stature within the Chamber of Commerce. By 1928, ambitious plans to aid working women and a motto aimed at heightening their civic reputation uncharacteristically appeared in the Division's monthly page. The women announced their loyalties to the senior chamber with the motto "Boosting Without Boasting" and cautioned fellow members against criticism of the organization. This allegiance to the Chamber's agenda conflicted with newly conceived programs, such as a planned day nursery and monthly luncheon programs in downtown tea rooms, which clearly sought the support of working women and delved into gender self-help. The new president, Eula Lang, a single professional woman, also urged members to join the electorate. "As the central woman's civic organization of Atlanta," she wrote, "it is our desire that our members be very active in exercising the right to a voice in governmental management."[68] With new leadership and a new agenda, the Women's Division seemed poised to enter civic territory unexplored by working women.

Between 1930 and 1936, gender self-help and political awareness lost momentum as the organization launched several programs to aid the unemployed and those seeking relief from the Depression. Through these programs, the Women's Division interacted more frequently with other women's groups, particularly the YWCA and the Business and Professional Women's Club of Atlanta (BPWC), but it did not aim its relief programs specifically toward working women. The relief campaigns, in conjunction with the Emergency Relief Commission, collected food and clothing for needy families.[69] The Division collected pennies and held rummage sales to add to its relief treasury. Christmas gifts were distributed at parties held every year for the children at Battle Hill Sanitorium. Toys were collected and repaired, utilizing the unemployed, and then sold to provide further benefits. In January 1932, the Woman's Division claimed 412 families were assisted.

Throughout the early Depression years, the Division struggled to maintain its identity and viability as a business women's organization. In 1930, Regina Corrigan, a department manager for First National

Bank, took the helm of the Division. She boasted that despite the economic difficulties suffered by working women, the organization maintained a membership of 200 women. Mildred Seydell, a popular columnist for the Atlanta *Georgian*, chaired a new committee formed to assemble statistics on Atlanta business women. The Division sponsored classes in Advertising and Commercial Art, stressed the importance of voting, and began a scrapbook featuring prominent business and professional women. Recognizing the strains placed upon working women in the 1930s, monthly luncheon meetings, a recent expansion, were trimmed to quarterly gatherings and an installment dues payment plan was implemented.[70]

Throughout the early 1930s, the Women's Division continued to appropriate political roles for women and promote women's economic and civic contributions to the city. Most of the Division's occupational propaganda took the form of Seydell's survey, which failed to inform or quantify working women's accomplishments, but gave business women good press. Adopting the tactics used by male civic leaders, the Division boosted its own breed, adopting language and imagery popular in business presses. In 1935, the Division debuted a new feature in its monthly column, "Atlanta Woman City Builders." This column highlighted business women's organizational activities throughout the city. The large women's clubs, such as the BPWC, the YWCA, and the Atlanta Women's Club received singular attention through feature stories. On its eighth anniversary, the annual National Business Women's Week, sponsored by the Atlanta Business and Professional Women's Club, received its first notice on the pages of the *City Builder.*

The following year, the senior Chamber of Commerce discontinued publication of the *City Builder* and resorted to a scaled-down mimeographed newsletter. In 1937, the Women's Division, which always strived to be financially independent from the senior, applied for a charter from the Fulton County Superior Court. Between 1937 and 1940, the Division's activities are unknown. In 1940, the Atlanta Women's Chamber of Commerce emerged as a weakened organization that discussed in vague terms its difficult separation from the senior Chamber. By 1943, the Women's Chamber slowly started to rebuild its organization with twenty-five active members and a $700 yearly budget.[71]

In its early years, the Women's Division played a minor role in civic affairs as cultural purveyors for the business class. It essentially served as a women's auxiliary to the Atlanta Chamber of Commerce. In this dependent position, the Division accepted a submissive female role characteristic of many contemporary Atlanta women's organizations. The Chamber and Division relationship also implied an organizational loyalty that affected the Division's ability to promote other less traditional women's clubs activities. By appealing to housewives to enlarge its organization, the Division diminished the importance of issues directly related to business and professional women, who comprised its membership. The civic efforts undertaken by the Division in this period are noteworthy, but they failed to address the social and cultural concerns of business women.

Despite the initial dependence of the Division upon the Chamber throughout the 1920s, it strove to change by expanding its activities, extending membership to the increasing white-collar female workforce, and joining national federation networks. At its inception, the Women's Division had been indistinguishable from the plethora of secular, elitist women's clubs that dominated Atlanta women's civic involvement. The Depression and a growing consciousness among its members challenged the Division to adopt a female civic identity.

Atlanta's civic organizations influenced the lives of white-collar working women in several ways through outwardly reformist goals and more subtle cultural change. The city's civic network reflected Atlanta's power structure and how women as individuals and through organizations operated within a male-dominated civic community. The Atlanta Chamber of Commerce and the business community at-large promoted programs that would enhance the city's economic growth. Vocational training through public funding, characterized in the expanded business curricula of the public schools and the Opportunity School, directly benefited the city's growing commercial economy and its dominant business-civic class. As a large laboring group, white-collar women broadly participated in and benefited from these educational programs and city-wide employment placement agencies. Within and outside the male civic community, the Women's Chamber of Commerce and the YWCA pursued similar programs to aid white-collar working women. They promoted increased educational opportunities, provided training, scholarships, or living accommodations and most importantly, strove to promote the business woman as citizen. The goals of these women's organizations reflected the fitful beginnings of a gender-centric approach to community and economic participation among business women. Later organizations, particularly the Business & Professional Women's Club, would expand the definition of business women's culture.

NOTES

1. Garofalo, "Business Ideas in Atlanta," 44-46.

2. Blaine Brownell, "The Commercial-Civic Elite and City Planning in Atlanta, Memphis, and New Orleans in the 1920s," *Journal of Southern History* XLI, 3 (May 1975):350-351.

3. Ibid., 345-347, 357-360, 363, 365.

4. Garofalo, "Business Ideas in Atlanta," 106-108.

5. Brownell, "Civic-Commercial Elite," 365.

6. Morrell Heald, "Business Thought in the Twenties: Social Responsibility," *American Quarterly* 13 (1961):127-128.

7. *City Builder* (September, 1922):31.

8. *City Builder* (April, 1922); Garofalo, "Business Ideas in Atlanta," 51, 94-96.

9. Phillip N. Racine, "Atlanta's Schools: A History of the Public School System 1869-1955" (Ph.D. diss., Emory University, 1969), 1-3, 14, 33-34.

10. Racine, 64, 78-79; Melvin W. Ecke, *From Ivy Street to Kennedy Center: Centennial History of the Atlanta Public School System* (Atlanta Board of Education, 1972), 46.

11. Timothy J. Crimmins, "The Crystal Stair: A Study of the Effects of Class, Race, and Ethnicity on Secondary Education in Atlanta, 1872-1925" (Ph.D. diss., Emory University, 1972), 70, 88, 212. The author posits that small working-class student enrollment resulted more from text book costs and the irrelevancy of classical educations for working-class girls than a conscious educational policy decision.

12. See Janice Harriet Weiss, "Educating for Clerical Work: A History of Commercial Education in the U.S. Since 1850" (Ed.D. diss., Harvard University, 1978).

13. Board of Education Minutes, 29 June 1889, 58-59 in Ecke, 42.

14. Crimmins, "The Crystal Stair," 162, upper-class student enrollment, decreased from 30 percent in 1881 to 17 percent in 1896, and middle-class student enrollment increased from 61 percent to 75 percent.

15. Mrs. C. J. McElheny, "The History of Commercial High School and its Significance" (Masters Thesis, Ogelthorpe University, 1935), 2, 4, 9.

16. McElheny, 2, 5.

17. Eighteenth Annual Report of the Atlanta Board of Education, 1890, 16-17; Twenty-third Annual Report of the Atlanta Board of Education, 1894;

"The Saga of a Business Girl in the 1890s" in S.W. and Elizabeth H. McCallie Papers, Atlanta Historical Society.

18. Garofalo, "Business Ideas in Atlanta," 124-129; Janice Harriet Weiss, "Educating for Clerical Work: A History of Commercial Education in the United States since 1850" (Ed.D., diss., Harvard University, 1978) Chapter 3, passim. Weiss notes that businessmen generally were not interested in the education level of their employees; that commercial education stemmed from educators' efforts. I would agree that educators initiated the trend, for reasons of support, but businessmen surely advanced public business training programs.

19. DeVault, "Sons and Daughters", 150; Janice Harriet Weiss, "Educating for Clerical Work: A History of Commercial Education in the United States since 1850" (Ed.D. diss., Harvard University, 1978), 55-57, 60.

20. "The Crichton Method of Shorthand: A Course of Study in the Crichton College, Atlanta, Ga." Handbook, n.d. (c. 1925), Crichton Business College Records, MS 623, Georgia Department of Archives and History, Atlanta.

21. Crimmins, "Crystal Stair," 183. Girls High Collection, 1936-1939 Reunion, Atlanta Historical Society Library and Archives. Although not a reliable sample, former students filled out biographical questionnaires and many Girls High graduates enrolled in private business schools after high school. Educational requirements among business concerns are explored through the office work survey. Questionnaires, Atlanta Office Work Survey, (1934) Women's Bureau, U.S. Department of Labor, RG 86, National Archives.

22. Crimmins, "The Crystal Stair," 158.

23. Racine, "Atlanta's Schools," 148-149; Ecke, 92, 173.

24. *Girls High Times*, 1938, Girls High School Collection, Atlanta Historical Society.

25. Racine, 91.

26. Ecke, 58, 74-75, 106; Personal files of Walter Bell, Archivist, Atlanta Board of Education Archives.

27. David Gordon, Richard Edwards, and Michael Reich, *Segmented Work, Divided Workers: The Historic Transformation of Labor in the United States* (Cambridge: Cambridge University Press, 1982), 203.

28. Weiss, "Educating for Clerical Work," 182.

29. Myrtle Belle Durham, "History of the Atlanta Opportunity School" (Masters Thesis, Emory University, 1938), 6, 12. Durham mentions opportunity schools in rural Georgia, Denver, and New York City. The name "Opportunity School" was borrowed from Denver's vocational extra-curricular school programs. South Carolina also sponsored an Opportunity School see William

Gray, et.al., *The Opportunity Schools of South Carolina: An Experimental Study* (New York: American Association for Adult Education, 1932).

30. Ada Virginia Colvin, "The Atlanta Opportunity School," *City Builder* 8, no. 6 (August, 1923): 40.

31. Ecke, 193. The Strayer-Engelhart Report also recommended the creation of Junior High Schools to provide educational opportunities to those students unlikely to attend the senior high schools.

32. *Atlanta Public School Directory*, 1927, 36. Mary C. Barker Collection, Special Collections, Woodruff Library, Emory University.

33. Lota W. Orr, "Opportunity School Observes Eleventh Anniversary," *City Builder* 17 (March 1932): 14. Durham summarizes age range of students between the years 1921 and 1928. The majority of students fell between the ages of sixteen and twenty-six with women enrolled outnumbering men two to one.

34. Durham, 14-15, 27, 92.

35. Durham, 95-103.

36. Durham, 29, 32-40. Cator Woolford, President of Retail Credit Company was one of many influential supporters.

37. Douglas Fleming, "Atlanta, the Depression, and the New Deal" (Ph.D. diss., Emory University, 1984), 45; Garofalo, "Business Ideas in Atlanta," 180; Ecke, 221-222.

38. Racine, 265-266, 268-270; Ecke, 271-272.

39. Racine, 268-275.

40. Willis A. Sutton, "Business and Education" *NEA Proceedings*, 1941, 278.

41. Ecke, 222.

42. Willis A. Sutton, "Problems of a Superintendent" *NEA Proceedings*, 1937, 75; "Problems in Education" *NEA Proceedings*, 1931, 69.

43. Young Women's Christian Association, Board of Director Meeting Minutes, 7 April 1905 and 25 September 1907, ADS, YWCA Collection, Special Collections, Woodruff Library, Emory University, Atlanta.

44. "Twenty-five Years of Service to Atlanta's Unemployed", TMs, 20 May 1940, Equifax Company Files, Atlanta.

45. "Twenty-five Years of Service to Atlanta's Unemployed," passim.

46. YWCA Board of Director Meeting Minutes, 1919-1922, YWCA Collection, Woodruff Library, Emory University, Atlanta. In 1922, 249 applicants sought work and 85 were placed, raising the success rate to 34 percent, a noticeable improvement.

47. YWCA Board of Director Meeting Minutes, 1923.

48. "The Consolidated Employment Service" *City Builder*, March 1923, 8: 18-19.

49. YWCA Board of Director Meeting Minutes, 22 July 1926.

50. "Taking Care of the Unemployed" *City Builder*, August 1927: 36. Roy LeCraw, future mayor of Atlanta, served as the President of the Atlanta CES in 1927. In the same article, LeCraw suggested training unskilled white women for domestic work "since here is a field into which white girls and women could go and make considerably more money than they can as salesgirls and factory workers." He further suggested that black female domestics made more money than unskilled white women and had better living conditions. It's not hard to imagine why the CES fared poorly in its initial years.

51. Anne Firor Scott, *Making the Invisible Woman Visible* (Urbana: University of Illinois, 1984), 215-217. Mary R. Beard examines women's work in the early twentieth century and will be outlined in a later chapter. See Mary R. Beard, *Women's Work in Municipalities* (National Municipal League Monograph Series, 1915; repr., New York: Arno Press, 1972); see also Anne Firor Scott, *The Southern Lady: From Pedestal to Politics, 1830-1930* (Chicago: University of Chicago Press, 1970) for a general discussion of southern women's organizational activities.

52. Darlene Roth, "Matronage: Patterns in Women's Organizations, Atlanta, Georgia, 1890-1940", (Ph. D. diss., George Washington University, 1978), 384-385.

53. Roth, "Matronage", 22, 32.

54. Scott, *The Southern Lady*, 144-148.

55. Board of Director Meeting Minutes, Atlanta YWCA, 1903 and 1904, Special Collections, Woodruff Library, Emory University, Atlanta.

56. Anne Lavinia Branch, "Atlanta and the American Settlement House Movement" (Masters Thesis, Emory University, 1966), 41-44 and; Jacqueline Rouse, *Lugenia Burns Hope, Black Southern Reformer* (Athens: University of Georgia Press, 1989), 25-30, 65-68.

57. "National League for Women's Service", *City Builder*, 10 July 1917, 13.

58. *City Builder*, June 1919, 18.

59. Board of Director Meeting Minutes, Atlanta YWCA, 1903-1917, Special Collections, Woodruff Library, Emory University, Atlanta. For an excellent discussion of industrial working women in Atlanta see, Gretchen Erhman Maclachlan, "Women's Work: Atlanta's Industrialization and Urbanization, 1879-1929" (Ph.D. diss., Emory University, 1992.)

60. Mary Frederickson, "Citizens for Democracy: The Industrial Programs of the YWCA" in Joyce Kornbluh and Mary Frederickson, eds., *Sisterhood and*

Solidarity: Workers Education for Women, 1914-1984 (Philadelphia: Temple University Press, 1984), 77-78.

61. "Business women" and thus, business clubs is a very ambiguous term used by editors, churches, businessmen, and the women themselves. It includes more than clerical workers, but definitely excludes industrial or manual working women. This leaves a rather broad group: sales clerks, clerical workers, teachers, nurses, professionals, even entrepreneurs. It is easy to read "clerical worker" for "business woman", but that would be an unsubstantiated assumption. If the language used implied office workers, I will specify clerical workers. Again, this is subjective, but working women in this large white collar group did not always identified themselves as typists, stenographers, or clerks. Nurses and teachers often joined professional organizations very specific to their occupations and they can usually be identified more clearly.

62. Lisa Fine, "'The Record Keepers of Property': The Making of the Female Clerical Labor Force in Chicago, 1870-1930," (Ph. D. diss., University of Wisconsin-Madison, 1985), Chapter 4, passim.

63. Scharf, *To Work and to Wed*, 15. A more detailed analysis of Atlanta business women's club membership is presented in Chapter Five.

64. *City Builder*, August 1921, September 1922.

65. Susie Wailes, "What the Women's Division of the Chamber of Commerce Means to Atlanta," *City Builder* 8 (May 1923):35-37.

66. *City Builder*, "Woman's Division" (February 1925): 35; *City Builder*, "Woman's Division" (April 1928): 29.

67. *City Builder*, "Woman's Division" (June 1927): 26.

68. *City Builder*, "Woman's Division" (June 1928): 32; *City Builder*, "Woman's Division" (August 1928): 25; *City Builder*, "Woman's Division" (December 1928): 24.

69. *City Builder*, "Woman's Division" (April 1931): 24.

70. *City Builder*, "Woman's Division" (January 1930): 30; *City Builder*, "Woman's Division" (December 1930); *City Builder*, "Woman's Division" (February 1930): 21; *City Builder*, "Woman's Division" (January 1932): 19; *City Builder*, "Woman's Division" (February 1932): 14.

71. Woman's Chamber of Commerce Collection, Board of Director Meeting Minutes, 1 October 1940, 21 April 1942, 18 January 1943, TMs, Atlanta Historical Society Library.

CHAPTER 5

Businesswomen's Idealism: Civicism and the Clerical Worker

Women have always been naturally idealistic and always will be, but the difference between their present and past idealism lies in the fact that today it is more far-reaching, extending to the interests of their neighbors and the community at large.

Mary Beard, 1915[1]

Mary Beard's research of women's social welfare activities in the nation's largest cities revealed that women were active reforming many issues related to American life including: education, public health, recreation, the assimilation of races, housing, social services, corrections, public safety, and general civic improvement. The middle- and upper-class female social reformers Beard studied focused their programs upon the poor and particularly the female poor. The settlement house movement, modeled after Jane Addams' Hull House in Chicago, remains the most poignant and successful example of women's urban reform measures.

In the South, women's social welfare activities typically began in the Protestant churches, especially among the Methodist and Presbyterian sects. It eventually branched out to secular women's clubs as these clubs gained popular acceptance.[2] Atlanta churchwomen established one of the first settlement houses for industrial workers at the Fulton Bag and Cotton Mill in 1902, primarily to provide medical care to workers struck by an influenza epidemic. The advent of secular women's clubs in the 1890s broadened women's reform activities beyond church-sponsored aid and attempted to address municipal-wide civic concerns. The Atlanta Young Women's Christian Association (YWCA) sought to engage Christian women in welfare work that transcended the domain of typical church-sponsored domestic missions and served a multi-faith, even nonreligious, needy urban community. Through organizations like the YWCA, and later the Women's Division of the Atlanta Chamber of Commerce, southern urban women also lobbied for female vocational education in the city's schools, citywide and national suffrage, and expanded city services to the poor.

Not all of Atlanta women's clubs engaged in social welfare work. The most prominent clubs largely functioned as socially active nerve centers for the female elite. These clubwomen created a network predicated upon the ideals of good motherhood and a sexually segregated society that was independent of church affiliations and traditional women's eleemosynary activities. The clubs supported liberal and conservative causes, both the status quo and change-oriented issues within a female network of social associations. Darlene Roth dubbed this network a Female Establishment and coined the term "matronage" to define this feminine social order.[3]

Roth studied only the most socially prominent clubs that belonged to the large secular and religious Atlanta female club network. But nearly every Protestant church had a woman's auxiliary. Composed of female church members organized in prayer circles, these auxiliaries raised money for domestic and foreign charities and added significant contributions to church building funds. Like secular women's clubs, the church circles also afforded their members the opportunity to meet other women who often shared social class, and invariably race, and provided a forum for these women to create socially gratifying and significant community-service networks within the comfort of their gender. Male civic and church leadership considered these women's auxiliaries innocuous although they wielded considerable power among their memberships and also contributed significantly to an expanding role of "women's work" within municipalities.

The women's missionary auxiliaries tended to be much more catholic than the network of secular women's clubs. Prerequisites such as church memberships and good community standing broadened the scope of possible members beyond the socially elevated. Their activities also concentrated more pointedly on their duty to community and God. Although considered secondary to male church leadership, the women's auxiliaries commonly acted independently, serving the needs of their members as well as the goals of their churches. Conducted within the confines of the church, women's municipal welfare activities achieved considerable influence and social sanction.[4]

Between 1895 and World War I, secular women's clubs greatly expanded. The Atlanta *Constitution* regularly reported the activities of prominent wives and daughters and their social gatherings, weddings, and community-service projects. Elite women created a female club establishment centered on social and charitable activities that were typically clustered geographically but more importantly composed an expansive female club society. One of the largest secular city clubs, the Atlanta Women's Club (AWC), accepted members from throughout the city and served as a model of community service and social status for other emerging women's clubs. The activities of the AWC, established in 1895, covered an entire page in the Sunday social section. In the press, the club's charity drives and bridge parties shared equal importance. At the height of its popularity, the AWC counted 788 active members.[5]

In the post-World War I period, another group of women's organizations joined the ranks of secular and religious women's clubs and auxiliaries. Business and professional women formed clubs wherein they publicly proclaimed their primary identity as working women; a significant departure from existing female club affiliations that linked women by social class or religious beliefs. By forming these organizations, business and professional women hoped to broaden the role women traditionally played in civic affairs through their social or religious organizations and to garner respect and recognition for the growing business women's community. Although organizations like the Atlanta Women's Club or the Daughters of the American Revolution remained the largest and most popular social-civic organizations in early twentieth-century Atlanta, newfledged business women's clubs gained legitimacy among both working women and professional women.[6]

The earliest female professional organizations, the National League of Nursing Education and the American Nurses Association, emerged from the Chicago World's Columbian Exposition held in 1893. These organizations sought to enroll women on an occupational basis and advocate better nursing education. Some associations, like the Federation of Teachers, affiliated with the American Federation of Labor (AFL), in an effort to command better wages and working conditions, as well as recognition of their professionalism. Despite their majority in the profession, female teachers could not join the AFL until 1918 when classroom teachers were admitted as members.[7]

The business and professional women's clubs also sought recognition of their professional status and advocated better education and career opportunities for women. They rarely organized in response to unfair labor conditions or solely to gain professional peer acceptance as other working women's groups did. Instead, they sought recognition as members of an urban business community and aspired to integrate women's talents into civic activities.

Numerous business and professional women's clubs simultaneously emerged after the United States entered World War I. The war affected women's organizations through patriotic appeals that called women to duty in a variety of activities and spurred existing women's clubs to band together. By 1918, the National Federation of Women's Clubs mobilized existing Federation clubs and shifted their activities to war work. Lacking a national organization, business and professional women felt underutilized during the war, even though over 105 business and professional women's clubs existed nationally.[8] At war's end, business women felt compelled to establish a centralized federation.

A national organization of business and professional women germinated after a meeting held in New York in May 1918. The National Board of the YWCA sponsored a gathering of more than one hundred white-collar women specifically to aid the war effort. The National YWCA had allocated funds granted by the War Work Council to various business and professional women's clubs and other women's organizations, often through local or state YWCAs. Lena Madesin Phillips, a lawyer from Nicholasville, Kentucky, served with the Kentucky YWCA, and because of her efforts there, the National YWCA appointed her Business Women's Secretary, charged with business women's war work. Phillips arranged the first YWCA-sponsored business and professional women's gathering in New York.[9]

Through subsequent travel among business women, Phillips concluded that these women wanted to form a national organization independent of the YWCA. Many business women agreed that the organizational requirements of the YWCA would limit the goals of business women, in war work and beyond. The diversity of business women, politically, religiously, and socially, would never mesh with the YWCA which, although progressive, was dominated at the local level by elite female officers and depended upon businessmen and municipal governments for patronage. Sensing an opportunity for change, Phillips requested that the YWCA Business Women's Committee be allowed to attend the National Convention of the Women's Association of Commerce, scheduled to meet in St. Louis in February 1919. Joined by YWCA members and independent business women, Phillips established the National Federation of Business and Professional Women's Clubs.[10]

Several founders of the National Federation of Business and Professional Women's Clubs (BPWCs) actively performed civic service through their local women's associations of commerce. This link heightened business women's awareness of the constraints imposed by financial obligation to a male business-civic consortium or through auxiliary status within a male organization. The BPWCs sought to assume leadership roles, formulate policy, and make decisions concerning women's working lives independent of direct male authority. Although most Atlanta women's clubs operated within female spheres, the civic roles they assumed never breached the entrenched male civic domain. The cultural improvement programs assumed by women's organizations like the Women's Division characterized the popular notion of female civicism during the 1920s and 1930s. The BPWCs' desire for financial independence set them apart. By acting autonomously, the BPWCs could establish their own agendas based on working women's needs and not feel indebted to political or social interests detrimental to their membership. These women assumed that advancing women's educational opportunities was the best place to start.

"BETTER BUSINESS WOMEN FOR A BETTER BUSINESS WORLD"

The Georgia Federation of BPWCs was formed in Atlanta in 1919 and within a year, clubs from Savannah, Athens, and Augusta met to discuss their activities. Although the Atlanta BPWC did not formally organize until November 1921, under the sponsorship of Lena Madesin Phillips, Stella Akin of Savannah, and Mrs. E. W. Carroll of Athens, Atlanta business and professional women attended the first two Georgia Federation meetings. By 1930, the twelfth annual Georgia Federation convention demonstrated that the BPWC had grown considerably. With clubs in Albany, Atlanta, Augusta, Bainbridge, Gainesville, Macon,

Millen, Moultrie, Savannah, Thomasville, and Valdosta, business women were everywhere.[11]

Almost immediately after its organization, the BPWC established itself as the business women's advocate. The National Federation of BPWCs' slogan for 1923, "A High School Education for Every Business Girl", recognized an issue that significantly affected female clerical workers' occupational advancement. Female clerical employment experienced dramatic growth in the 1920s, and many employers sought women with rudimentary educations to fill the lowest-ranked office positions. Commonly, general clerks performed the most menial tasks associated with office work such as opening mail, filing, and machine operation. Women who attended business courses, either through public high school programs or private business schools, often would enter office work in the clerk position and work their way up to stenographer and typist, if they possessed the skill. Such readily available entry-level employment, with limited required skills, prompted many women to quit school and go to work.

> I went to Girls High about 1916, but I did not graduate. I was a sophomore and I had the flu, or just beginning my third year. I had a very bad case and had two relapses, so I never went back to my books. But in the summertime, I took a six weeks course in shorthand at the old Commercial High School. It [the shorthand course] only had sixteen word signs. I saw an ad in the paper for an office worker for a one-man insurance company. I could take shorthand and answer the telephone. I typed with two fingers. Eventually, I learned to type with all my fingers but I always liked these two mostly. I think I must have been seventeen. [I worked] because we [her family] were hungry and Dad worked on commission and I couldn't just sit around the house. Besides I had these two relapses and I lost almost a whole year and I never got back to my books. It was a chance to get a job, so I got it.[12]

Women who entered office work during or immediately after World War I, before high school business curricula became commonplace, unwittingly participated in hiring practices that pigeonholed women into low-skill, low-paying positions that characterized female office work opportunities. The BPWC, and other groups like the Southern Woman's Educational Alliance, founded in Richmond, Virginia, urged young women to train themselves suitably for their selected occupations.[13] Nearly a decade after the National Federation of BPWCs proposed its agenda, the educational levels of Atlanta female office workers had improved, but not greatly. In 1931, the Women's Bureau studied Atlanta female office workers and reported that less than half of the women performing office work had completed high school. Secretarial, stenographic, correspondent, and supervisory positions had the highest completion rates. But approximately 50 percent of the city's female mail order clerks never went beyond grammar school.[14]

The proliferation of private schools and businessmen's efforts to promote extracurricular business training courses, like the Opportunity School, did not encourage young women seeking office employment to complete high school. The Women's Division of the Atlanta Chamber of Commerce, which possessed significant links to the business-civic elite and had a sizable membership, recognized that its efforts to strengthen women's business education programs would be futile because so many other training options were available. High school completion rates among clerical workers did not significantly increase until the Depression forced many undereducated women out of the workforce. Although the Atlanta BPWC adopted the slogan of the National Federation, its ambition to influence business women's education was hampered by the club's size. Thus, the first decade of club organization focused on enlarging club membership and expanding the state Federation territory.

The competition was fierce. At least five professional women's club organizations emerged nationally in the years immediately following World War I, and all eventually created Atlanta chapters. Three clubs appeared nationally in 1919. The Altrusa Club, organized in Nashville, Tennessee, limited its membership to female professionals, executives, or entrepreneurs. The Quota International Club, formed in Buffalo, New York, characterized itself as a business-service club and granted membership only to professional women. The Zonta Club also limited its membership to female professionals. The Soroptomist, organized in 1921, accepted professional and businesswomen at the executive level. Pilot International, also formed in 1921, broadened its membership beyond executives, but maintained tight control over who it admitted. By the 1930s, these clubs had established branches in Atlanta, and like the Atlanta BPWC, held membership in the National Federation of BPWCs.[15]

Many of the professional clubs, which excluded female clerical and retail sales workers, described themselves primarily as service clubs and secondarily as professional organizations. The Macon Pilot Club limited its memberships to "the most intelligent and earnest portion of the business or professional women of each community." This club went further by accepting "only those women whose social and business standing is unquestioned and who are leaders in their special lines [of work]."[16] Initially, only two women from each business or professional classification were chosen as Pilot members. This exclusivity sharply limited the club's ability to address the concerns of working women.

The Pilot Club's charter insisted that all members support themselves through employment. If marriage interfered with a woman's independent position, the individual forfeited her Pilot membership. No housewives, mothers, or independently wealthy patrons were offered active membership. However, women engaged in civic service, but without a professional or business income, could become associate members.[17] Pilot members, although working women, represented an occupational elite.

In 1941, the Pilot conducted a survey among business women in Cleveland, Ohio. Many of the women surveyed were indifferent to or uninterested in Pilot membership. They cited the abundance of other clubs, the burden of paying dues, the lack of youthful activities in the Pilot Club, and especially, the club's exclusivity as primary reasons for their lack of interest. "If you find any women that are eligible [for your club]," one woman laughingly replied, "let me hear from you."[18] Because of its exclusionary membership criteria, the Pilot Club rarely endeavored to embrace the ordinary, white-collar female.

Other women's professional clubs, like Zonta, Quota, and Soroptomist, also limited their memberships to the elite among working women and appeared largely indifferent to professional or other white-collar work-related issues. Most of the professional women's clubs maintained a close, and often dependent, relationship with their city's Chamber of Commerce and performed social-civic services unrelated to their peer group. They engaged most vigorously in charitable fundraising, hospital auxiliary work, and support for the arts. Occasionally, the clubs also contributed to the education of young women who wanted to attend normal school or business courses. Like the Pilot, these clubs had an exclusive membership and a civic-service agenda that discouraged much discourse on female occupational dilemmas.

The Atlanta BPWC membership policy represented a significant departure from clubs like the Pilot. The Atlanta club included clerical and retail workers as well as executives and professionals and opened its membership to all business women upon recommendation from a club member. This policy resulted in a high turnover rate, but also created a diversified membership that afforded recognition of the city's female white-collar population.

Throughout the 1920s, the Atlanta BPWC focused on enlarging the club's membership. In 1922, the Atlanta club listed thirty-one women as charter members. Several of these women held memberships in the Women's Division of the Chamber of Commerce and remained with the club throughout most of their adult careers. The Atlanta club increased to fifty-five members by 1923, and retained twelve of the original members. The 1927 membership remained stable at fifty-four members with sixteen women continuing their membership from 1923. By the end of the decade, the Atlanta BPWC had reached a plateau; seventy-four women were members. Fifty-one women had maintained their memberships from 1927 through 1929. This growth rate and stability remained unparalleled until the worst of the Depression had passed.[19]

The Atlanta club membership was diverse, but the most stable members were predominantly upper-level clerical workers, managers, or professionals. For the purposes of this study, three major groups of white-collar female workers are defined: low-level clerical workers; management/upper-level clerical workers; and professionals. Low-level clerical workers performed duties that tended to be routine and afforded little opportunity for advancement. They held positions such as typist, stenographer, bookkeeper, secretary (not private), machine operator, and clerk. Upper-level clerical workers consisted of cashiers, private secretaries, and accountants. Management and upper-level clerical work commonly overlapped in senior clerk and supervisory positions. Most female managers supervised all-female departments. Finally, professionals usually received some specific training and included: teachers, nurses, social workers, librarians, lawyers, and doctors.

Several other classes of female workers joined the Atlanta BPWC, but their representation was small. These women worked as retail clerks, retail merchandise buyers, insurance agents, proprietors, and executive officers. Professionals, managers, and executive officers dominated the club's offices, particularly the president and first and second vice-president positions. Upper-level clerical workers and several ambitious, and frequently young, low-level clerical workers held the lesser offices of treasurer, recording secretary, and corresponding secretary. The club's executive offices changed yearly, but remained dominated by long-standing, professional members. The lower offices, particularly recording secretary and treasurer, frequently retained the incumbent for several terms.[20]

Throughout 1927-1929, low-level clerical workers and management/upper-level clerical workers maintained an even representation in the club. In the club year 1927-28, the club sponsored eleven lower-level clerical workers and fourteen management/upper-level members. By 1929-30, twenty lower-level clerical workers held memberships and nineteen women representing management/upper-level positions paid their dues. Of the women who maintained memberships through 1927-1929, sixteen held management/upper-level clerical positions, ten worked in lower-level positions, and six were professionals.[21]

By 1935, the club's occupational representation had shifted. Out of seventy-eight members, low-level clerical workers made up the largest group (26), followed by managers and upper-level clerical workers (10) and proprietors and professionals (9). Low-level clerical workers also maintained the greatest longevity between 1929 and 1935. Nine out of twenty-seven club members who retained their memberships for six years were secretaries, typists, clerks, or bookkeepers. This trend continued throughout the 1930s. By 1939-40, low-level clerical workers represented nearly half of the club's membership (54), which reached a decadal high of 121 members.[22]

Table 5.1: Occupational Status, Atlanta BPWC Membership[23]

Status	Year			
	1927-28	1929-30	1935	1939-40
Low-level Clerical	11	20	26	54
Managers/Upper-level Clerical	14	19	10	14
Proprietors/ Professionals	8	8	9	8

The Atlanta BPWC's diverse membership signaled a change in the way women organized. Nineteenth-century women's clubs, like those studied by Roth, were homogenous socially, racially, and even geographically. Because few of their members worked, these clubs rarely addressed the concerns of labor. New organizations like the Pilot and Quota continued the tradition set by older women's clubs and maintained elite memberships, but as professional associations, these clubs occasionally entered employment-centered debates. The BPWCs broke new ground for women's organizations. Although separatist in their occupational interests, racially exclusive, and often sharing similar social class, the new generation of women's clubs did not strive to be elitist. Hierarchies of rank surely emerged, especially in office-holding and committee positions, but the clubs hoped to appeal to a variety of members through broadened club activities.[24]

Although clubs with predominantly elite, nonworking female memberships continued to prosper, many of the newer women's clubs would not be defined as elite social clubs. Increasingly, the General Federation of Women's Clubs included organizations like the BPWCs, and the term clubwoman lost some of its social distinctiveness. As working women entered clubs, fewer women identified themselves as career clubwomen. The social status conferred through the club hierarchy diminished and was replaced by professional or occupational rank.

One good example of the shift in clubwomen's identity lay in the club-as-home idea. Club homes represented a considerable monetary investment for individual clubs and reflected the organization's social position and feminine identification. The Atlanta Women's Club (AWC) purchased a former residence on Peachtree Street for use as a club headquarters. This large residence reflected the club's elite social status, geographic identity, and a distinct affiliation with women in the home, despite whatever nondomestic activities occurred there. Business women's clubs rarely purchased a club home, a common practice among women's social-civic clubs like the DAR or the AWC. Instead, business women's clubs met in hotels or civic auditoriums for two reasons. Primarily, as working women, business club members could not devote the administrative time required for operating a club house or residence. Secondarily, meeting in hotels, country clubs, and civic auditoriums separated businesswomen's club activities from their domestic roles, a distinction that was imperative to their acceptance within the male business-civic community.[25]

Despite the outwardly confident, business-like appearance engendered by meeting in downtown hotels, like the Georgian Terrace, the Atlanta BPWC membership committee lured members to monthly meetings by minimizing the importance of business functions and highlighting the evening's entertainment value. Club dues, which remained constant throughout the 1930s at fifteen dollars annually, paid for the Federation dues and meeting entertainment and dinner. These monthly meetings were not well attended, and the membership committee chairwoman frequently cajoled members to take an active interest in their club.

Like most civic clubs, the Atlanta BPWC also maintained rooms downtown for day use and invited business women to relax there, read the National Federation's publication, *The Independent Woman*, and meet with other women. Although no direct evidence is available indicating the age of Atlanta BPWC members, the club frequently urged it members to engage in physical activity at the YWCA's gymnasium and pool also located downtown. Occasionally, some club members would attend the YWCA's Camp Highland during the summer. The YWCA sponsored these activities for young, single working women, usually in their twenties.

The club calendar year revolved around the National Business Women's Week (NBWW), established by the National Federation in 1928. Generally held in March or April, the NBWW helped local clubs forge alliances with their business communities, and through increased media exposure, the week's activities invariably increased membership. The first NBWW coincided with the premiere issue of the Atlanta club's monthly newsletter, *Flashlights*, which strove to interest its members in the Federation's agenda. Initially, *Flashlights* reported the events of the NBWW, Federation news, and urged members to attend meetings and help expand the club's membership. Throughout the 1930s, however, the newsletter adopted a more political tone in response to the heightened assault upon business women's work opportunities.

"BOOST AND PREPARE WITH CONFIDENCE (BPWC)"

When the Atlanta club adopted this slogan in 1935, it had already joined a national campaign mounted to thwart congressional legislation that discriminated against working women. Section 213 of the 1932 Economy Act passed both the House and the Senate nestled in the folds of a much-needed omnibus bill that included appropriations for a public works administration, a department of national defense, provisions for veterans, and other government personnel salary details. Section 213, popularly known as "the married person clause," originated in the House Subcommittee on Appropriations to Executive Departments. It stipulated that whenever reductions in personnel occurred in the executive branch, married persons with spouses also in government service, would be discharged first. Because women's salaries rarely equaled or exceeded men's salaries, the bill, which intended to reduce executive department personnel, placed the onus of unemployment upon married women.[26]

Although opposition to the bill within the Senate existed, the budget was sorely needed, and a reluctant President Herbert Hoover signed the bill. Upon signing, Hoover added a censure of Section 213 and expressed a hope that the next session of Congress would eliminate the discriminatory clause. It didn't, and for five years, women's groups throughout the country lobbied for repeal of the clause in the face of the public's overwhelming support of the measure.[27]

The response of women's groups to Section 213 has been characterized by scholars as a revival of feminism after the post-suffrage lull. These scholars have studied the activities of the National Women's Party and women active in the Roosevelt administration to illustrate the mood of women during this occupational assault. Most women's groups concerned with female occupational opportunities strongly opposed the bill, but their motives were not always rooted in political activism. This bill clearly jeopardized an advance made by white-collar women: the increasing acceptance of married women workers. Through the efforts of several national women's organizations, especially the BPWCs, local women's clubs campaigned vigorously to abolish the discriminatory clause. The widespread economic consequences of Section 213 prompted women in local business women's clubs to support national agendas aimed at repeal even though these campaigns demanded confrontations with municipal and state officials, whose support they had attempted to nurture through the NBWW. Most women's organizations realized that failure to oppose a federal policy that discriminated against married women would condone the passage of similar laws at the state, county, and municipal levels. Frequently, local nepotism laws affected all married women even if their spouses did not hold government positions and severely limited all women's ability to contribute to their families.[28]

In Atlanta, two attempts, in 1932 and 1935, were made to exclude married women teachers from the city school system. Through a combined effort by the Atlanta BPWC and the Women's Division of the Chamber of Commerce, both measures were defeated. Neither the city nor the metropolitan counties attempted to exclude married women from government service again.[29]

Through its newsletter, *Flashlights*, the Atlanta BPWC strongly opposed Section 213 and embraced the National Federation's campaign to repeal the measure. Prior to this national hue and cry, Atlanta BPWC members rarely addressed the problem of discrimination against married women workers. This may have stemmed from the apparent tolerance of Atlanta employers toward married women workers noted by the Women's Bureau (see Chapter 2). Married women's participation in club membership often paralleled their participation in the city's white-collar workforce. In 1929-30, married women composed 23 percent of the club's membership, comparable to their overall participation in the city's white-collar workforce (27 percent). By 1936, one year before Section 213 was repealed, the club sponsored 32 new members, at least seven of whom were married.[30] The Atlanta BPWC's interest in abolishing discriminatory legislation represented then, not just pro forma commitment to the National Federation, but an agenda vital to the club's membership.

For many working women, Section 213 threatened dire economic consequences, and working club women unanimously supported its repeal. However, great debate erupted among the same club women concerning the support of the Equal Rights Amendment (ERA), sponsored by the National Women's Party (NWP). This debate was not parochial, but extended across many women's organizations and widened the ideological schism between political feminists, many of them professionals, and all other women's organizations.

Introduced in 1923 by the NWP, the amendment proposed to eliminate all unequal treatment between the sexes. As the measure's sole supporter until 1937, the NWP faced fierce opposition to the amendment by women's organizations, which felt it threatened existing protective legislation for women workers. Put on the defensive, the NWP stated that protective legislation was paternalistic and patronizing toward women workers because it further isolated them based on sex. The amendment's clearest benefits, the NWP claimed, lay in expanding women's legal status, which frequently subjugated women to male kin. Women's labor organizations that supported protective legislation roundly criticized the NWP for clinging to an abstract notion of sexual equality during an economic crisis that wounded many laboring women and their right to work. This stalemate reigned until the National Federation of BPWCs broke the deadlock in 1937 and supported the amendment. The subsequent passage of the Social Security Act and the Fair Labor Standards Act in 1938 diminished the protective legislation argument, but most female labor leaders remained opposed to the measure.[31]

The Atlanta BPWC unequivocally supported the abolition of Section 213, but was less unified over the ERA. The unquestionable link to women's economic independence and livelihood inherent in labor legislation dominated the *Flashlights* editions throughout 1935 and 1936. Atlanta club President Flora Ozburn echoed the National Federation's views drafted at the biennial convention in Seattle in July 1935 in her regular column: " we believe that aptitude, training, and efficiency should govern the securing or retaining of all employment and the opportunities of advancement . . . [and oppose] all legislation, business customs and policy which discriminates against the business and professional woman including the clerical classification."[32] This issue stimulated interest among the Atlanta club's membership and increased attendance at monthly meetings. The National Federation and the Atlanta club attempted to capitalize on their members' heightened interest in political process spurred by the ERA and Section 213 debates and sponsored agendas on "Effective Democracy" and "Creative Citizenship." The Federation's slogan, "The Business Woman as Citizen" urged club members "to enroll in political parties, vote at primary and general elections, . . . and to oppose actively all legislation and practices which discriminate against the employment of women by federal, state, county, or municipal governments."[33]

Atlanta club members received far less guidance from either the National Federation or their own officers concerning the passage of the ERA. In February, 1937, the Federation urged all clubs to study Senate Joint Resolution No. 1, called the Lucretia Mott Amendment (or the ERA). Little support for the measure existed outside of the Federation and the NWP. Both the Women's Bureau and the League of Women Voters (LOWV) declined to endorse the amendment. The LOWV described the measure's feminist supporters, primarily the NWP, and their tactics as "aggressive and intensely personal," and likely to arouse antagonism against women's interests. Despite the legal implications of the amendment's passage, the LOWV felt that "habits of thought" could not be changed by an amendment to the Constitution. Both the Women's Bureau and the LOWV agreed that the ERA would nullify protective legislation for women in industry and stated that business and professional women should not engage in campaigns that would jeopardize these advances made by industrial working women. If female business and professional workers wanted to advance their occupational opportunities, anti-ERA activists suggested, they should do so within their own organizations. These statements clearly established two camps: those who would support the ERA and thereby jeopardize the gains made for wage-earning female workers, and those who would support the status quo and protect hard-fought labor gains.[34]

The Atlanta club's diverse membership needed more guidance. Between 1935 and 1939, women working for salaries in clerical and retail positions composed over half of the club membership. They recognized the threat Section 213 posed for them as workers, especially in a depressed economy, and supported its repeal. But to risk one's livelihood to support an ambiguous ideal of social sexual equality was far less acceptable. As the LOWV declared, challenging the paternalistic and patronizing habits of business through the amendment would not guarantee wage-earning women better opportunities. Despite some attempts by professional club members to stress the importance of equalizing male and female legal rights, the Atlanta club's president urged members to utilize their femininity to change attitudes in the business world.

> Throughout history, notions have been swayed by the moral standards of women. We may be pioneering in some of the fields, the "hand that rocks the cradle" might also find it expedient to do other things, but we do not need to use the masculine pick ax and shovel on our frontiers. Let's do the job the woman's way and prove to the world it is a better way.
>
> Above all, do not let equal rights make a man of you. Retain your feminine charm![35]

After several months of coverage, the debates over the equal rights issue disappeared.

The role President Ozburn recommended to her membership represented a middle ground frequented by many working women during the 1920s and the 1930s. The 1920s witnessed the liberalization of social attitudes about women's work, suffrage, and even birth control. Conversely, a revival of domestic women's culture that aimed to return women to the home also distinguished the decade. The prosperity of urban centers in the 1920s opened economic opportunities for women and introduced a popular culture centered on working women. Movies, magazines, novels, and fashion catered to the newfangled "business girl." Concurrently, scientific theories on child-rearing, food preparation, and household management urged educated, middle-class women to return to the home.[36] The Depression greatly diminished the mounting popular acceptance of working women, especially married women, and despite the independence afforded by a business or professional career, most women preferred to marry and leave the workforce to raise a family.[37] President Ozburn recognized that many of her members worked for economic security before, during, and after marriage and that only a few personally identified with career feminism. Her advice to members to maintain their femininity acknowledged the majority opinion that women still held greatest influence within their domestic roles.

The Atlanta club participated in other less political, but equally vital, women's issues. The club recognized the need to provide recreational activities for business girls, often in concert with the YWCA. Few existing businesswomen's organizations addressed the mental and physical costs of low-level clerical or retail work. The YWCA, because it adopted a determined campaign to aid industrial working women, quickly recognized the demoralizing effects of the long working hours, mental and physical inactivity, and poverty that frequently plagued working women. The YWCA gymnasium and pool, Camp Highland in the summer, and the recreational weekday evening activities provided well-chaperoned physical stimulation for many young business girls.

The Atlanta BPWC also recognized the detrimental effects the work environment could have upon business women. In 1937, the Health Committee produced a series of articles in preparation for the annual NBWW that focused on the office environment and women's work. Noisy working conditions, endured especially by typists in large pools, or by women who worked among office machines, clearly affected women's ability to concentrate. The committee quoted a study that concluded that typists working under noisy conditions used 19 percent more energy and lost more than 4 percent in speed. At Western Union, installation of quieting equipment in a telephone room resulted in a net savings of 3 percent in the cost of messages and reduced handling errors by 42 percent. Ambient noise, whether produced within the office or outside of it, greatly affected clerical workers' efficiency.[38]

In 1931, the Women's Bureau studied several aspects of clerical workers' office conditions. Proper ventilation in pre-air-conditioned offices relied primarily on windows, and a few concerns installed electric fans, mostly portable. Many offices used natural light unsupplemented by artificial illumination. Women who needed more light sat near windows. Employers rarely provided restrooms specifically for their employees, but relied on those provided by the buildings they occupied. The Women's Bureau faulted employers for not providing matrons at restrooms. The utility companies received the highest marks for office environments. They routinely provided good ventilation, proper lighting, and used sound-proofing material to reduce the noise levels in large rooms.[39]

Women working in downtown Atlanta offices also suffered from street noises and airborne pollution. The Atlanta BPWC began a campaign in 1935 to address the issue of smoke and noise in the city. Led by long-term member Leita Thompson, the Smoke and Noise Abatement Committee linked the city's environment to the general health of its citizens and its female workers. As a railroad center, Atlanta suffered serious effects produced by coal-burning engines operating on the numerous rail lines that converged on the city's center at Five Points. In addition, the use of residential coal furnaces and noise emanating from dense automobile congestion greatly contributed to the sooty appearance and cacophony that pervaded downtown Atlanta. Several plans to reduce the effects of the smoky railroad gulch in 1923 through the construction of a great mall never materialized. However, in that same year construction on the Spring Street viaduct began, followed by others at Central and Pryor. These viaducts provided safe conveyance for automobiles and pedestrians over at-grade railroad tracks, but failed to reduce the smoke and noise levels in the city.[40] By 1937, Thompson's committee had gained the support of the Atlanta *Journal* and the Atlanta Board of Education to sponsor a public forum on this issue. Preparing for the forum, Thompson clarified the club's purpose and tactics.

> As I explained, our plan is not to institute drastic steps to stop the smoke and noise, but through a program of education acquaint the men and women of Atlanta with the many simple things than can be done to help and to arouse in them the desire to do their part.[41]

Thompson followed the forum with an avalanche of information on the proper use of coal furnaces. Several radio programs followed, sponsored by WSB, an affiliate of the Atlanta *Journal*, and the club ordered hundreds of brochures from the Appalachian Coal Company, which outlined the method for smokeless coal firing for distribution among Atlanta school children.

Thompson realized that the campaign to reduce the city's sooty appearance was a large one and she chose a tactic that would offer the least offense to both city residents and commercial interests. After studying the problem, Thompson and city Smoke Inspector A. W. Jones concluded that unregulated residential furnaces and coal-burning railroad switching engines were the dirtiest culprits. A 1935 city ordinance placed some restrictions on businesses and manufacturing establishments that emitted smoke, but the residential and railroad offenders polluted without censure. The radio programs and brochures addressed the residential problem, but initially, neither Thompson nor the city confronted transportation officials. Railroads served the city's manufacturing and distribution industries, and any threats to this industry could cripple the city's regional dominance.

Returning from a trip, Atlanta BPWC member Dr. Maude Foster wrote to Thompson with her ideas on smoke abatement. Atlanta Terminal Station, she wrote, was "belching filth as usual." Foster urged Thompson to utilize the city newspapers to publicize the inaction of the worst offenders. "The papers are so committedly on our side," she wrote, "I believe they'd print such a series if you asked them." But Foster added, in a moment of sober reality, "forget it if it seems wiser to."[42] Taking the lead in this controversial issue had awed Thompson, not only because of its enormity, but also because many powerful municipal interests could be antagonized.

Late in 1938, city officials and businessmen called a conference of railroad interests to reduce the smoke emitted in the city. Earlier in the year, a modest but powerful effort by BPWC clubwoman Odessa Henson helped motivate these reformers. Henson held a position at Rich's department store as private secretary to Frank Neely, Vice President. In a memo, Henson presented the club's idea of a united business approach toward convincing the railroads to convert to diesel engines within the city. Neely approved of the idea and gave his support to the BPWC's effort.[43]

Eventually, the city Sanitation Department, the Atlanta *Journal* and *Constitution*, the Atlanta Real Estate Board, and the Atlanta Retail

Merchants Association lobbied for diesel engine use in the city. By January 1940, the BPWC announced that the existing city smoke ordinances would be revised and strengthened to include restrictions on residences and other coal-burning industries. Unlike other issues supported by the Atlanta BPWC during the 1920s and the 1930s, the smoke abatement campaign characterizes the methods business women used to achieve civic improvements and yet retain the support of the urban community.

THE WOMEN'S NETWORK

Contemporary with the Atlanta BPWC and other business and professional clubs, another layer of women's clubs, some of which touched the lives of business women, also existed. The Women's Division of the Chamber of Commerce, the Atlanta YWCA, and church-sponsored business women's circles actively encouraged business women to become members, but these organizations had decidedly different memberships and agendas.

Church-sponsored business women circles originated in the women's auxiliaries of Atlanta Protestant churches. Second Ponce de Leon Baptist supported the oldest and largest business women's circle, counting 160 active members in 1930. Begun in 1913 by Mrs. Frederic Paxon, wife of a prominent Atlanta retail merchant, the Business Women's League (BWL) consisted of working women church members. These women belonged to a large network of Southern Baptist women's auxiliaries called the Atlanta Association of Baptist Women. In 1927, sixty-four societies operated in Atlanta alone. Traditionally, women's auxiliaries raised money for domestic and foreign missions and church-building activities. The BWL prodigiously raised funds, collecting $120,198 in sixteen years (1914-1929).[44]

"Business women" was an ambiguous term among church circles. Because women's auxiliaries commonly met during the business day, working women were often excluded from the most prominent women's activities available within the churches. Business women's prayer circles emerged in response to the increasing number of active female church members who worked. What type of work these women performed is unclear. However, in a church like Second Baptist, originally located downtown in the business district, female church members came from both prominent families and the wage-earning class. Any female church member could belong to a circle, and the

BWL provided an opportunity for all churchwomen to participate in Christian fellowship among themselves and with the community.

Most of the funds collected by the BWL went directly to the church, but as economic conditions worsened throughout the 1930s, the League's activities turned increasingly towards the Community Chest, sponsoring relief work and finding jobs for the unemployed. The single self-serving activity the League supported was the establishment of an endowment fund to provide a room and medical services at the Georgia Baptist Hospital for working women. Many League members delivered their children at the hospital in the room provided by the endowment. The League created a second benevolent fund for business women incapacitated by illness, who lost time and wages from their jobs.[45]

The scope of the business women's circles among Protestant churches is unknown, but their potential to influence white-collar working women was enormous. Within the Central Presbyterian Church, a large Women's Auxiliary operated to succor and support church members and fund missionary activities. The Central Presbyterian's business women's circle began in 1923, and by 1927 had named itself the Annie Crusoe Club. The club formed within the Young Women's Bible Class, which had helped initiate a business women's boarding home, the Annie Crusoe Home. By 1923, the Women's Auxiliary welcomed the business women's circle into their auxiliary network. Most of the circles within Central Presbyterian were small, averaging fifteen to twenty members.[46]

Within eleven years, the business women of Central Presbyterian had formed two circles within the Women's Auxiliary, but because of the size of these circles, businesswomen nearly composed a separate auxiliary. In 1934-35, five circles within the Auxiliary reported their activities in an annual report. Circles one through three each possessed approximately fifty members with an average of fifteen to twenty active participants. The business women's circles had 138 and 72 members respectively and counted 68 active participants. By 1938, Business Women's Circle No. One enrolled 208 members with an average meeting attendance of thirty-nine women.[47]

Central Presbyterian's business women's circles and women's auxiliary circles performed similar activities, but the business women's circles frequently grew because of defections from the other circles. By 1938, the two business women's circles composed over half of the 410 members of the eleven circles in the Women's Auxiliary. There are two likely reasons for this growth. Business women's circles often met immediately after church services on Sunday or on Saturdays in members' homes. The women's auxiliaries as frequently met on weekday mornings or afternoons. Secondly, the Central Presbyterian business women's circles devoted a considerable portion of their meetings to modest secular entertainments. In 1935, Business Women's Circle No. One held two pageants and two outdoor picnic meetings and repeatedly sponsored vocal performances and speakers from the YWCA. Members described business women's circle meetings as "both interesting and attractive." The other circles within the auxiliary with smaller memberships rarely garnered speakers or vocal performers.[48]

The activities of business women's circles in both Central Presbyterian and Second Baptist represented a significant association for business women, a number who would have been white-collar workers. Although largely spiritual in origin, these organizations clearly illustrated the expanding importance of a distinct business women's identity.

Both the Atlanta YWCA and the Women's Division of the Chamber of Commerce preceded the BPWC as the only women's organizations that specifically recognized working women and developed activities directed toward them. Within the Women's Division, membership among working women represented an occupational elite. Overwhelmingly, entrepreneurs, managers, and professionals occupied the membership rosters of the Division, although some clerical workers did enroll. The Women's Division's close financial association until 1937 with the senior Chamber of Commerce also limited its effectiveness as a working women's organization. The Division's endeavors focused mainly on women's role as cultural standard bearers; secondly as citizens responsible for domesticated civic duty, such as the clean-up campaigns and tree plantings; and finally as business women who should take interest in other working women, exemplified most pointedly in the various campaigns to support the Churches Homes (residences for young working women), establish a day nursery, and complete surveys on businessmen's attitudes toward working women.

Through its column in the *City Builder*, the Women's Division publicized the events of the organization, but its activities and advocacy oriented toward working women lacked boldness and were largely ineffective. Burdened with a feminine role and a powerful patron, the Division could not participate in meaningful advocacy. Throughout the

1920s and 1930s, the Women's Division never outgrew its auxiliary status.

The YWCA provided many more services for working women within its organization, but these often focused on a transient clientele and required the acceptance of decidedly middle-class social and moral standards. The YWCA, as the acronym suggests, served the needs of youthful female wage earners. Through the SISP and Clover Clubs and the residences, business "girls" had a distinctive place in the Y, albeit a well-chaperoned one. In the broadest terms, the YWCA provided young business women earning low salaries an economical place to live, moral and religious instruction, some vocational training, an employment bureau, recreational facilities, and companionship. For young women arriving alone from small towns or rural areas, the Y was a reliable place within the city.

Although young business women benefited from YWCA services, the association reserved its labor advocacy for industrial working women and lent mostly moral support and guidance to young, white-collar working women. The residence homes and the employment bureau helped many young women seeking clerical employment, and the Business Girls League maintained the highest membership of all the YWCA intraclub activities. The YWCA promoted its residence on Baker Street as homelike, so much so that its boarders frequently left to be married. "It is my opinion," the residence matron supplied, "that marriage might never have come about if it were not for the utter homelikeness of the Y."[49] For young women who did not marry, the YWCA residences often served merely as way stations, places to start and sometimes end their clerical work careers in Atlanta.

> There are girls who go from city to city, working their way in order to see the country. In Atlanta, they usually locate the YWCA Home and there they are counselled until they voluntarily return to their homes.[50]

The YWCA also functioned as a moral exemplar for the community and operated its residences within that standard. For clerical workers, the YWCA represented an improvement over other inexpensive housing alternatives available in the city, namely the Churches Homes for Girls. One journalist wrote that the YWCA homes provided "the freedom of a hotel with a club-like atmosphere, and home-like also."[51] The Churches Homes, with six establishments in

1921, could claim that "no girls in the city are more carefully chaperoned" than those at the residences. The home mother often accompanied girls to the theater and other places of amusement. The price of freedom varied for working girls. The Churches Homes provided room and board for $2.45 a week and was intended for girls earning the lowest wages, for some as low as $10 a week; at the YWCA, $4.75 paid for a shared room and board and for $7 a girl could have her own room. If an average salary for a stenographer in the early 1930s was $75 a month, a room of one's own could be dear.[52]

At both the YWCA and the Churches Homes, prospective boarders needed to pass a litmus test of character. "Of course, no girl of questionable character is taken in; the homes are not rescue homes in any sense."[53] The rigors of this qualification likely differed among the residences, but at the Churches Homes, unemployment did not diminish a young woman's character. The YWCA was not so generous and would persuade women without prospects to return home or go to the Churches Homes. At the YWCA, a young woman had to be able to afford $20 from her monthly salary to stay.

Grace Hutchins criticized the YWCA as an elitist organization, administered by wealthy wives and supported by the business elite, that failed to advance the interests of young working women.[54] This conflict of interest, Hutchins wrote, limited the YWCA's ability to raise working women's occupational standards. Although the YWCA supported young business women, it rarely addressed the problems these working women faced on the job. The Atlanta YWCA and the Churches Homes focused their attention on the moral health and safety of young, single business girls and industrial workers. The perceived perils facing young women, especially those without families, at public workplaces and in their residences, dictated the programs established for business women on the national and local level. The residences, established to be homelike and as centers for wholesome recreation, illustrate well the YWCA's primary concerns for working women. The YWCA also strove to solve the problems young business women experienced at work by providing "good homes" and religious and moral instruction. Atlanta employers, like the Retail Credit Company, agreed that girls from good homes imbued with solid moral judgement made better employees.

> She was a good typist, but she was constantly having scenes with her
> fellow workers. Her employer asked the YW what to do as he needed

her work. She was introduced to a group of Y girls and there she learned the value of friendship, consideration of others, and the value of companionship.[55]

Despite the enlarged emphasis on moral probity, the YWCA adjoined with the Works Projects Administration in 1934 to promote business women's labor education. The Workers' Education Program issued from the successful Southern Summer Schools for Women Workers in Industry and federal relief programs aimed at unemployed teachers. The Federal Policy Guidelines for Workers' Education authorized on September 26, 1933, stated that "the purpose [of the program] is to stimulate an active and continued interest in the economic problems of our times and to develop a sense of responsibility."[56] The Affiliated Schools for Workers, Atlanta Project sponsored an opportunity for working women to attend educational classes without having to compete for scholarships or take time absent from their work. The program lasted for ten weeks, between March 26 and June 1, 1934, and invited primarily industrial working women to attend. The YWCA, both the white and black branches, sent numerous young women to attend.

Four distinct groups represented the YWCA: the Industrial Girls from the black branch and the Business Girls, Industrial Girls, and Southern Bell Girls from the white branch. The classes were racially segregated and divided by occupational interests. By the second week of classes, the business girls group had grown, meeting twice a week in the evenings.[57]

The classes held in Atlanta in the summer of 1934 introduced YWCA members to their role within the American economy. Although English, Current Events, and Economics shared equal class time, the young industrial women attending classes objected most strongly to the discussions of hours and wages, current business conditions, and social reform measures, particularly the growing anti-lynching sentiment among southern women. Mostly, the women feared that what they perceived as the radical nature of wage and hour and social conscience issues would affect their employment. But members of the YWCA business clubs voiced little opposition to the tenor of these discussions, which frequently borrowed from labor organizing techniques. However, the Southern Bell employees, a firm-specific YWCA business club, reacted quite strongly to the radical nature of the classes and eventually stopped attending. The students believed that government should not interfere with business conditions. Their teacher felt assured that this sentiment was "the attitude of big business and especially [of] the Southern Bell."[58]

The YWCA encouraged young business and industrial women to attend the various summer sessions held throughout the Depression despite some community reprobation. Mary C. Barker, chairman of the Committee on Worker's Education, received a veiled threat from the Fulton County Federal Reserve Relief office, which administered the educational program in Georgia. Numerous prominent citizens had criticized the workers' education program and sought the county's support to discontinue the project. Barker's curt reply quoted Federal Emergency Relief Administration guidelines that allowed for "complete freedom of teaching and discussion."[59] The matter was promptly dropped.

Despite the varied agendas and memberships represented within the Women's Division of the Chamber of Commerce, the Atlanta YWCA, and the Atlanta BPWC, all of these women's organizations strove to engage business women in the problems and solutions of their city and their gender. The Women's Division drew members from a mixed community of working and elite women and leaned heavily upon businessmen's support. The YWCA, although national in scope, frequently called upon local elite women to sponsor community projects. These groups performed services that linked working women with the elite community in a substantial way. Both the Women's Division and the YWCA incorporated female civicism within their own memberships and expanded the civic ideal among business women. But these organizations, germinated in the soil of traditional women's activities, remained subject to the male-dominated business-civic power structure through direct patronage or implied duty.

The Atlanta BPWC and the church-sponsored business women's circles operated in distinct and yet shared ways. The BPWC's sexual political awareness and advocacy clearly isolated them from the more domesticated women's network. Yet, the BPWC and the church circles both adopted a business women's identity appropriate for their environments. As a civic business women's club, the BPWC openly proclaimed its allegiance to working women. As church members and business women, circle participants enacted their social duties within acceptable limits, but held steadfast to the badge of business woman, despite what its implications might be.

NOTES

1. Mary Beard, *Women's Work in Municipalities* (National Municipal League Monograph Series, 1915; repr. New York: Arno Press, 1972), 306.

2. Scott, *The Southern Lady*, 142, 150 and Anne Lavinia Branch, "Atlanta and the American Settlement House Movement" (Masters thesis, Emory University, 1966), passim.

3. Roth, "Matronage," 11.

4. Nationally, Dorothy Brown addresses the role women played in church missions during the 1920s. She notes that male-dominated general missionary boards emerged in the early 1920s, especially among the Presbytery, and began to replace the autonomous missionary societies created and operated by churchwomen. This trend affected southern women's roles in the churches also but was not particularly pronounced during the 1920s and the 1930s or among the Baptists who operated foreign and domestic missions within the individual churches and not through centralized boards; Dorothy Brown, *Setting a Course: American Women in the 1920s* (Boston: Twayne Publishers, 1987), 168-172.

5. Atlanta Women's Club, Yearbook, Members 1926-27, Subject File, Atlanta History Center (AHC).

6. The United Daughters of the Confederacy, the Daughters of the American Revolution, and the Colonial Dames, as studied by Darlene Roth, were primarily hereditary associations, but they served social and civic functions as well.

7. Sophinisba P. Breckinridge, *Women in the Twentieth Century: A Study of Their Political, Social, and Economic Activities* (New York: McGraw-Hill Book Company, Inc., 1933), 24.

8. Breckinridge, 37, 40, 42.

9. Leita Thompson, "The Organization of the National Federation of Business and Professional Women's Clubs," *Flashlights* 7, no. 3 (May 1934): 7; located in Atlanta BPWC Records, uncatalogued collection, Georgia Department of Archives and History, Atlanta, hereafter cited as Atlanta BPWC.

10. Ibid, 8.

11. "For Those Who Do Not Know," TMs, n. d., Miscellaneous Records, Financial Statements, and Histories and Annual Reports, Atlanta BPWC; Leita Thompson, "A History of the Georgia Federation of Business and Professional Women's Clubs Inc., May 1919-May 1956," TMs, April 1957, Atlanta BPWC.

12. Mrs. Jessie Cowan, interview with author, 19 September 1989, Tape recording, Atlanta, Georgia.

13. The Southern Women's Educational Alliance, "The Girl and Her Ambition," pamphlet, n. d., Subject File, AHC. Founded in 1919, the Alliance

served primarily as an information source. By the late 1920s, it directed its information services largely toward women's advanced education and training for professional careers in nursing and social work, hoping to influence women to seek alternatives to clerical work.

14. Erickson, "Women Who Work in Offices," 60.

15. Breckinridge, 37-39.

16. Pilot Club Papers, Box 1, Georgia Department of Archives and History, Atlanta.

17. Constitution of Pilot Club of Atlanta: As Amended, October 10, 1939, in 1939 Yearbook, Subject File, AHC.

18. Daily Reports, Field Work, 1941, Pilot Club Papers.

19. Membership list, TL, 19 January 1922, Membership List, TD, 1922, Statement of Club Membership, TD, 1927-1928, Membership Ledger 1927-1928, Membership Ledger 1929-1930, Box 2, Atlanta BPWC.

20. Darlene Roth notes in her study of Atlanta women's clubs that the presidency was held democratically by a number of women in the club, consisting of short terms. But the lesser offices, such as treasurer and secretary, were often held for several terms by the same individual. Roth, "Matronage," 167.

21. Membership Ledgers, 1927-1930, Atlanta BPWC.

22. Yearbook 1935, Roster, and Yearbook 1939-40, Roster, Box 2, Atlanta BPWC.

23. The years represented in the table were selected based on the comparable data available among the membership rosters located within the Atlanta BPWC manuscript collection. Several rosters for other years did not indicate status or were not complete annual rosters.

24. This expansiveness often resulted in a considerable lack of focus. By attempting to address the concerns of professionals and laboring women alike, the BPWCs frequently failed to advocate successfully for either group.

25. Breckinridge, 64, 84.

26. Scharf, 46.

27. Scharf, 47-48, 51; the author notes that "[r]egardless of demographic and geographic variables [public opinion polls] revealed that Americans were overwhelmingly opposed to the employment of married women."

28. Scharf, 51; The author describes the threat women felt to combining "marriage and career feminism" posed by Section 213. This may have been the rhetoric utilized by career feminists, but few working women, even within business women's clubs, personally identified with the political agendas of outspoken feminist organizations. Instead, as the Women's Bureau concluded, most married women worked because a single male income was not sufficient.

29. *Flashlights* 8, no. 3 (May 1935): 2-3, Atlanta BPWC.

30. Membership Ledger, 1929-1930; Kay Bland, "Our New Members," *Flashlights* 10, no. 7 (October, 1936): n.p. Full membership information for 1936 is not available, however, in 1935, 52 percent of the club's members were single; 6 percent identified themselves as widowed in the City Directory; the remaining 41 percent (32 out of 78 total members) were likely married.

31. Susan Ware, *Holding Their Own: American Women in the 1930s*, (Boston: Twayne Publishers, 1982), 107-108.

32. *Flashlights* 8, no. 6 (August 1935): 2, 5.

33. *Flashlights* 10, no. 3 (June 1936): 2-3; and 7 (October 1936): n.p.

34. *Flashlights* 10, no. 11 (February 1937): n.p.

35. *Flashlights* 10, no. 6 (September 1937): n.p.

36. See Dorothy M. Brown, *Setting a Course: American Women in the 1920s*; Anne Firor Scott also discusses the liberalization of popular culture during the 1920s and the advent of the "new woman"; see Scott, *Making the Invisible Woman Visible*, passim, 211-227. The *Atlanta Journal Sunday Magazine* throughout the 1920s carried articles, advice columns, department store advertisements, and short stories catered to the young business woman.

37. In *Women's Work and Family Values, 1920-1940*, Winifred D. Wandersee discusses at length women's impetus for working, most often citing statistics gathered through the Lynd's Middleton study. Throughout the 1920s, the Atlanta *Journal* and the Atlanta *Constitution* published articles that stressed the importance of women's domestic roles.

38. *Flashlights* 10, no. 12 (March 1937): 1.

39. Women's Bureau, Office Workers' Survey, "Working Conditions," General Interviews, May 1931.

40. Howard L. Preston, "A New Kind of Horizontal City: Automobility in Atlanta, 1900-1930" (Ph.D. diss., Emory University, 1974), 165, 168-69.

41. Leita Thompson to Mr. W. Cole Jones, Associate Editor of the Atlanta *Journal*, TL, 8 February 1937.

42. Maude Foster, M.D., to Leita Thompson, LS, no date (c. January 1938), Atlanta BPWC.

43. Odessa Henson to Leita Thompson, TLs, 13 December 1938, Atlanta BPWC.

44. *Second Baptist Church Yearbook*, 1930, 17-20, Second Ponce de Leon Baptist Church, hereafter cited as Second Baptist, Subject File, AHC. Originally known as Second Baptist Church and located across from the Capitol, the church changed its name to Second Ponce De Leon Baptist Church after a merger in 1932 with the Ponce De Leon Baptist Church. New construction near the Capitol forced the church to relocate. Also, many of its

members had moved away from the downtown residential area as office buildings and manufacturing interests located in the area.

45. Second Baptist Business Women's League, Annual Reports, 1930, 1932, 1933, 1934; *Second Baptist Church Yearbook*, 1930, "The Business Women's League," 17-18, Second Baptist, Subject File, AHC.

46. Axile Simpson, "Women's Work in Central Presbyterian Church of Atlanta, Georgia," TMs, Central Presbyterian Church Collection, hereafter cited as Central Presbyterian, AHC.

47. Annual Reports, Central Presbyterian Women's Auxiliary, 1933-1938, Central Presbyterian, AHC.

48. Annual Reports, Central Presbyterian Women's Auxiliary, 1935, 1938.

49. YWCA Atlanta Collection, Scrapbooks 1928-1930, Special Collections, Woodruff Library, Emory University, Atlanta.

50. "Permanent Quarters to be Opened in the Middle of September by YWCA," Atlanta *Journal* 14 September 1924, 16.

51. Medora Field, "Wanted: A Home, by the Business Girl," *Atlanta Journal Sunday Magazine*, 24 April 1921, 14.

52. "Churches Provide Real Homes for Working Girls," *Atlanta Journal Sunday Magazine*, 11 March 1923, 12.

53. Ibid.

54. Hutchins, *Women Who Work*, 256-257.

55. Atlanta *Journal*, 14 September 1924, 16.

56. Affiliated Schools for Workers, Atlanta Project, 1933-1934, "Federal Policy Guidelines," Folder 2, Mary C. Barker Collection, Special Collections, Woodruff Library, Emory University, Atlanta.

57. Affiliated Summer School Report, 1934, Atlanta Project, Mary C. Barker Collection.

58. Affiliated School for Workers, Atlanta Project, Staff Meeting Notes, 4 May 1934 and 12 May 1934, Mary C. Barker Collection.

59. Mary C. Barker, Chairman, Committee on Worker's Education to Miss Ada Barker, Administrator, Federal Reserve Relief for Fulton County, TL, 29 May 1934, Mary C. Barker Collection.

CHAPTER 6

Losing Ground

The Great Depression catapulted the nation into the direst economic conditions of the century and halted a decade of spectacular economic growth. In the South, remarkable physical growth reflected the economic optimism of the 1920s. Southern cities had expanded their industrial, manufacturing, and commercial economies greatly in the post-World War I boom. In Atlanta, office buildings and hotels replaced elite homes along Peachtree, the city's main artery; residential suburbs mushroomed and housed a growing urban white-collar class; and viaducts raised the new automobile street system high above the smoky railroad gulch that served as the metropolis's commercial lifeline. The city also expanded philosophically by vigorously adopting a pro-growth mentality. Boosterism embodied in the Forward Atlanta Movement touted the city's advantages to investors outside the metropolitan and regional limits. Growth and opportunity infused the Atlanta Spirit in the 1920s, and even the news of the stock market crash in late 1929 could not quickly squelch the booster spirit. By nearly all accounts, 1929 had been a record year, and many city leaders were reluctant to acknowledge that the good times may be ending.

Atlanta's diverse manufacturing, white-collar, and service workers suffered through the Depression in ways as disparate as their occupations. Those who remained employed lost many of the privileges they enjoyed during the twenties, especially the luxuries that middle-class prosperity afforded such as automobiles and movie-going. For the unemployed, the Depression exposed the needy to the humiliation of accepting the federal dole or meant total deprivation because even public emergency work or assistance did not reach them.

For Atlanta women, the degree of hardship caused by the Depression depended greatly upon race and varied profoundly among occupational groups. As manufacturing industries reduced production and workforces, women lost the gains they had achieved in manufacturing jobs during and after World War I, often losing their jobs for the sake of sustaining male employment. Professional women endured criticism and social censure, although unemployment among this class was low unless they directly competed with men. Black women, one of the city's largest female occupational groups, suffered a disproportionate share of unemployment, especially among the personal servant class. In laundries, hotels, and other service industries dominated by black labor, jobless whites increasingly pushed blacks out. Teachers and women in clerical occupations also brooked significant occupational setbacks manifested in shortened school years or lowered salaries. Faced with daunting circumstances, women and their families turned to creative means of support by engaging boarders, sending wives into the workforce to replace a lost male income, or seeking out relief.

Relief for needy women proved hard to initiate, and the federal administrators of women's work projects consistently fought off criticism. Although women had increased their paid workforce participation greatly in the postwar period, especially among clerical occupations and in manufacturing and light industry, many Americans still considered women's employment secondary to men's, despite working- and middle-class families' reliance on female incomes. For the majority of unskilled, unemployed, or never employed women, public works projects were not available. While the Civilian Conservation Corps (CCC) and the Civil Works Administration (CWA) put armies of unemployed men and male youths to work, women gathered in state and county welfare offices and in breadlines in their early attempts to keep their families fed. Destitute women who possessed no skills and sought relief had few options but direct relief. When work programs began in the winter of 1933, most women entered large sewing rooms established throughout rural and urban areas. Initially, federal relief program administrators felt overwhelmed by the female needy and responded by hastily establishing sewing projects to employ women. As women's relief projects grew, the federal response became more progressive and the administrators launched programs that employed skilled female white-collar workers and professionals.

HOW ATLANTA FARED, 1929-1933

After the initial shock of the crash, Atlanta businessmen reassured themselves and the citizenry of the economy's soundness by illustrating its stability and continued growth. Throughout the next two years, they optimistically reported that a few stores were making profits, some banks had indicated increased clearings, and monthly retail sales had advanced. In reality, the Atlanta economy was still sliding downward. Between 1929 and 1933, when federal relief programs began, building permits for new construction in Atlanta decreased from $27 million to less than $900,000. Three office building projects begun in 1929 were completed, but these were the last privately financed construction projects in the central city until after World War II. Housing construction literally halted, and those dwellings recently built often remained vacant. To economize and accommodate housing demand, homeowners and landlords subdivided older homes in areas like Inman Park, an 1890s-era elite residential suburb. Vacancy rates in the downtown office building market, significantly overbuilt throughout the 1920s, escalated to nearly 20 percent in 1931.[1]

Two other important areas of Atlanta's economy also suffered troubling setbacks between 1929 and 1933. Retail sales plummeted, forcing Chamberlin-Johnson-DuBose, a well-respected, high-quality department store, to close its doors. Rich's, another prominent local department store, also experienced heavy losses between 1930 and 1933, but was able to remain open.[2] The Davidson-Paxon Company, another locally owned store that had merged in 1925 with Macy's of New York, also remained solvent. Convention business dropped considerably. Much of the pre- and post-World War I building boom focused on hotels constructed for a rising convention trade. More than 81,075 businessmen and women attended conventions in the city in 1923. A decade later, the convention business had fallen to record lows with only 28,175 businessmen visiting the city.[3]

Despite these indications of remarkable economic decline, business leaders remained optimistic. The *City Builder* eschewed negative reports in favor of misleading growth indicators that intended to keep the city's spirits raised. The Chamber of Commerce publication reminded its business readership that the city had grown even when the surrounding countryside had experienced significant setbacks in the mid-twenties, caused by a devastating boll weevil infestation and the postwar decline in cotton prices. During those years, rural migrants found jobs in Atlanta's growing white-collar and manufacturing sectors. Those who could not find employment sought relief from private charitable agencies and the Community Chest. Because the city's growth had been so steady throughout the 1920s, Atlanta's city leaders and citizens entered the Depression years with high hopes.[4]

This sanguine attitude faded, however, when unemployment reached nearly 25 percent of the city's employable population by 1933. Throughout the Depression, southern urban unemployment frequently exceeded the national average of 25 percent, which inevitably caused southern cities to suffer more acutely than the densely populated, industrialized northern centers. In 1933, Atlanta and Birmingham had 33,000 and 25,000 relief cases representing 25 and 35 percent of their populations respectively. By comparison, Detroit and New York reported 8.5 and 15.5 percent of their populations receiving relief.[5] Although few southern cities with more than 100,000 inhabitants employed more than 40 percent of their workforce in industry—the economic sector most vulnerable to decline during the 1930s—the South still suffered great economic devastation, especially in agricultural areas. Despite exhortations by regional boosters to diversify agricultural production, southern farmers throughout the 1920s had continued to rely upon cotton, exhausting the soil and inuring the workforce to a landless indebtedness through sharecropping. As the boll weevil infestation spread throughout southern cotton growing regions, landless tenants migrated to cities and manufacturing centers looking for employment.[6] Southern urban populations swelled throughout the 1920s, and the prosperous urban economies often welcomed this largely unskilled class of workers. In Atlanta, textile manufacturing, domestic service, and some municipal public works projects absorbed the rural jobless during the 1920s.[7] But when the prosperity of the 1920s disappeared, and demand for manufactured goods plummeted, the unskilled found few opportunities in southern urban centers, which were largely dominated by nonindustrial occupations.

Unskilled men and women swelled the relief rolls in Atlanta in 1931 and 1932, but they found very little true relief. Despite a growing unskilled and jobless population evident throughout the late 1920s, Atlanta's municipal leaders failed to establish adequate publicly funded social service agencies and relied heavily on private charities. Until 1929, the combined effort of the city's churches and the Atlanta Community Chest had provided for the city's poor. The thirty-nine agencies included in the Community Chest aimed to raise $480,000 in 1929 for charity relief. After the crash, these agencies were overwhelmed by the massive need.[8]

The city's charitable agencies, dominated by conservative business interests and religious leaders, practiced fiscal conservatism and attempted to enforce morality among the poor by imposing character qualifications as a basis of need.[9] The fierce debate concerning movies shown on Sundays to raise funds for charity illustrates the tenacious hold conservative religious interests had over Atlanta's charitable agencies despite the desperate need of the poor.

The Evangelical Ministers Association (EMA) represented more than 120 Atlanta white Protestant churches and exercised considerable political and social influence. The EMA lamented the general decline in morality in the city and served as a watchdog for observance of Sunday blue laws, which restricted entertainments, such as movies and public dining. In 1931, the EMA complained that the Community Chest removed charitable functions from the churches into the hands of social service agencies.

> The churches lost the strongest hold they have ever had on the hearts and imaginations of the people of Atlanta when they allowed the administration of charity to pass into the hands of social service, non-religious organizations who administer relief in the name of humanity and civic pride. When a charity worker goes into a home, his or her visit should be for the glory of and in the name of Jesus Christ, and the christian churches are missing a glorious opportunity for christian salesmanship when they allow this work to be done on merely a business basis.[10]

When newly elected Mayor James Key supported "Sunday Movies for Charity" in 1931, he condoned the violation of state and municipal codes. The EMA waged a fierce campaign to abort what it considered to be a blasphemous practice. The ministers won and cut short a program that raised $1,500 each Sunday for the poor.[11]

Additional efforts by city leaders to provide relief also foundered. The Chamber of Commerce sponsored a program of agricultural resettlement in August 1932 that intended to equip unemployed city residents with farms, thereby reducing the number of needy citizens. The "back to the farm" program failed miserably. In the winter of 1932, the Atlanta Central Relief Committee provided modest work relief with municipal funds. However, the transient population flooding the city that winter quickly exhausted the Committee's small relief budget, and the homeless and jobless had no public relief assistance.[12] None of these efforts significantly improved the plight of the city's penniless.

The citizens hardest hit could least afford to lose their employment. Domestic workers, a class of predominantly black female workers with few alternative employment opportunities, constituted 25 percent of the 1930 Atlanta workforce. By 1934, domestic employment had dropped by one-quarter, and black women composed over 75 percent of the jobless (see Tables 6.1 and 6.2).

Table 6.1: Selected Occupations of Atlanta Women on Relief

Occupation	Number of Women	Percentage of Workforce
Professionals	70	0.8
Teachers	36	0.4
Nurses	7	—
Clerical	300	3.4
Bookkeepers	41	0.4
Clerks	70	0.8
Stenographers &Typists	190	2.0
Saleswomen	253	3.0
Textile Operatives	176	2.0
Domestic Servants	6352	74.0

Source: Katherine Wood, "Urban Workers on Relief, May 1934," *WPA Research Monograph No. 4.*

Compared to manufacturing and service workers, Atlanta's middle class, white-collar population faired well in the years following the crash. . In 1930, approximately 15 percent of Atlanta's employed population engaged in clerical occupations; another 7 percent were professionals; and 17.5 percent worked in retail and wholesale trade occupations (see Table 1.2.). The first urban relief statistics compiled by the Federal Emergency Relief Administration (FERA) in 1934 revealed that clerical workers suffered the least among white-collar occupations. Only 3 percent of the clerical workforce registered for relief, while nearly 10 percent of those engaged in trade sought assistance. Manufacturing and mechanical industries employed 25 percent of Atlanta's workers, and 16.6 percent of that workforce applied for relief in 1934 (see Table 6.2.)[13]

Table 6.2: Selected Occupations of Atlantans on Relief 1934

Occupation	1930 Census	Number on Relief 1934	1930 Population
Clerical	19,132	646	3.3
Professional Service	8,850	372	4.2
Trade	22,646	2,291	10
Manufacturing & Mechanical	32,147	5,346	16.6
Domestic Service	33,188	8,010	24.1

Source: Katherine Wood, "Urban Workers on Relief, May 1934," and U.S. Department of Commerce, *Fourteenth Census, 1930.*

Among white-collar employees, the Depression represented a reduction in the standard of living, but not substantial hardship. This was true in Atlanta and throughout the nation. Waged and salaried employees realized a remarkable increase in their standard of living immediately after World War I that was manifested in increased consumption habits and a reliance on convenience goods. The Depression curtailed a decade's worth of accumulation of material goods, debt assumption, and dependence on a money economy that accompanied the prolonged prosperity of the 1920s.[14]

Several technological trends had accelerated the elevation of wage and salaried workers' expectations: widespread use of electricity and running water, popularization of radio broadcasts and the automobile, and the commercial use of refrigerated trains and the goods they transported. All of these factors greatly enlarged the consumption habits of moderate-income families. Among these families, those with the highest incomes had chief earners who were semiskilled or clerical workers and lived in households with related adults and lodgers.[15]

For example, Marie Cooper, a legal secretary, shared her Atlanta home with her mother, her sister, and her brother-in-law. All of the adults worked except the mother, and with their combined incomes they maintained a high standard of living that included home ownership, a car, and a servant. Stella Brady worked as a typist and stenographer for the Atlanta PTA in the mid-1930s. Her salary supplemented her husband's small investment income and helped support her family in rural Georgia. "I was still helping my mother," Stella remembered; "she hadn't married again. I was still sending money [to her], so I went to work." Although she occasionally left the workforce and relied on her husband's income, Stella felt that working wives helped families stay together. " I don't think people would have made it if it wasn't for their wives. We had a hard time."[16]

A national study of wage and clerical workers' spending habits in the mid-1930s indicated that one-third of the families surveyed had supplementary earners, most frequently female, who contributed approximately one-third of the family income. In Richmond, the income of supplementary workers was large because women and girls could find work in tobacco factories. Two other southern cities examined, New Orleans and Birmingham, did not report significant supplementary female employment among families where the chief earner was a wage or low-salaried clerical worker.[17]

Comparative figures for Atlanta are not available, but in the early 1930s at least, the middle class and the elite maintained an active social and recreational life and "neither accepted permanent depression nor sought radical changes in the economic structure of their city."[18] The wage-earner and the low-salaried clerical worker likely experienced income cuts and job loss,[19] but family economies still afforded the pursuit of cheap popular entertainment and luxuries such as automobiles, newspapers, candy, and tobacco to many employed Atlanta residents. One reader wrote to Mildred Seydell, a local columnist for the Atlanta *Georgian* in 1931:

> People says it is hard time. And they are suffering for foods & clothing & Etc. But you can believe it or not, Last night at the Capitol and Georgia Theater I watched the line of people which blocked the sidewalk trying to buy a 60 cent ticket for the show. Also the ten cent store was so crowded with candy buyers you couldn't walk. Do you think there is any depression here if so please explain in your column. I think the biggest thing is talk.[20]

Despite the Depression, the employed middle-class, especially a large pool of working females, continued to purchase modest luxuries. For example, although men's clothing and shoe purchases slackened, demand remained high for women's clothing. Floral and book shops grew despite the Depression. New homes were not purchased or built throughout most of the 1930s, but middle-class Atlantans kept their cars and continued to take vacations. The terminally cheerful *City Builder* reported that,

Atlanta has not lost its sense of humor—we are still here—the stores are open and the trains are running. You can get your number on the telephone, we have a traffic problem, seats are hard to get in the theaters, doctors, and dentists make appointments weeks ahead, lawyers briefs are just as long.[21]

For Atlantans, the severity of the Depression depended greatly upon one's class and one's race and to some extent upon gender. Atlanta's black female service workers lost their jobs as white families learned to make do without additional help. Because black women in Atlanta had few occupational choices, their job losses forced them into the ranks of the unemployable.[22] Southern black men were largely excluded from early federally assisted construction projects despite increasing pressure from Washington to allocate relief regardless of race.[23] Unskilled women, many of them rural migrants, also suffered greatly whether they were white or black. Without marketable skills and with few jobs available, these women were forced to seek relief. Finally, the city's teachers, a predominately female laboring class, also experienced significant setbacks in the early years of the Depression because of Atlanta's fiscal insolvency. The city frequently paid its teachers in scrip, which few retailers accepted for full cash value, and also shortened the school year to limit expenses. Although employed, Atlanta's teachers lived with great uncertainty about their livelihoods.[24]

THE STATE OF RELIEF, 1933-1940

Meaningful relief for Atlanta's jobless did not materialize until federal relief programs were established. The city's weak relief apparatus crumbled under the dire need largely because the city failed to tax for the necessary funds and the business-civic elite never committed to progressive reforms. Although the city government contributed to Grady Hospital and to private charitable agencies—consolidated into the Community Chest in the late 1920s—it took little responsibility for Atlanta's indigent residents. For example, in the winters of 1929 and 1930 itinerants joined the city unemployed on the streets and compelled the mayor and the city council to initiate a "War on Beggars," instructing Police Chief Beavers to "keep the unemployed moving or at home," but city leaders offered little meaningful help.[25]

In May 1933, Congress responded to the national crisis by establishing the Federal Emergency Relief Administration (FERA), which operated through state-administered relief commissions and provided direct assistance and work relief. The Georgia Relief Commission administered the program through county relief apparatuses. Typically, urban areas garnered the largest proportion of relief funds and city dwellers received the most direct relief. County relief programs most often only offered work relief. In July 1933, when the Georgia Emergency Relief Administration began funding relief projects, with federal appropriations, Gay B. Shepperson, the director of the State Department of Public Welfare, became director of the Georgia Relief Commission (GRC). Shepperson attempted to administer federal funds through the GRC to the most needy, which often meant urban populations, and she encountered fierce opposition from Georgia Governor Eugene Talmage. In January 1934, Shepperson challenged Talmage's covert control of the federally funded GRC. Within a year, FERA director Harry Hopkins stepped in and federalized the Georgia Relief Commission, removing Governor Talmage altogether from the relief process. Georgia, Louisiana, and Kentucky were the only federalized relief agencies in 1935.[26]

Many southern relief programs administered by county and city governments employed women trained in social work. Shepperson's appointment riled Talmage because she was a woman; she ignored apportionment based on political patronage; and she had a larger budget than he controlled. Despite Talmage's protestations at federal intervention in the GRC and the appointment of Shepperson, she had de facto control over relief programs as the only trained relief administrator within the GRC.[27]

The FERA greatly improved the harsh conditions suffered by many Atlantans and Georgians by providing the state with funds to relieve dire poverty through work and direct relief. The FERA created the Civil Works Administration (CWA) in the winter of 1933 specifically to provide work relief for the coming winter, when relief rolls were expected to swell. In previous winters, southern urban relief agencies had strained under the burden of hundreds of indigent migrants seeking more hospitable climates. The FERA allocated funds to establish transient bureaus in cities nationwide in October 1933 to encourage the wandering jobless to settle in one place or to seek work in their city of origin. The CWA work relief employed mostly manual labor on street paving, construction, and beautification programs in DeKalb and Fulton counties, which encompassed Atlanta and adjacent urban areas such as Decatur, East Point, Hapeville, and College Park. Most of the FERA work relief programs operating in Georgia between 1933 and 1935 helped the state's urban populations and consisted of construction projects like those in Fulton and DeKalb counties.[28]

The CWA also engaged a significant number of unemployed females, establishing clerical projects for skilled women and sewing projects for the unskilled. Subsequent federal relief programs expanded the aid available for women. But providing female relief caused considerable difficulties for CWA and later Works Progress Administration (WPA) directors, because most public work relief required manual labor and was intended for men. Early work relief efforts harnessed labor and funding to construct schools, public buildings and hospitals, sewer systems, and roads. The female needy, especially the unskilled, were harder to serve. In rural areas, unskilled women dominated the needy ranks.

The CWA and the WPA placed skilled female workers in clerical work positions where they helped record and index deteriorating and unorganized county and city records, provided clerical assistance to public schools, and served as tabulators for federal statistical projects. The unskilled entered sewing rooms established in rural and urban areas and mended donated garments or created new clothes for individuals and families on relief. In the mid-1930s, the National Youth Administration (NYA) provided semi-skilled labor and training in book binding and library service to youths between sixteen and twenty-four years of age. The WPA also greatly expanded its training programs for unskilled women providing domestic science, childcare, hygiene, and some elementary education through adult education and literacy classes.

Despite the great need, early relief efforts in Atlanta served only approximately one-third of those that applied.[29] This limited success stemmed from the brevity and hastily implemented nature of the CWA projects. But without the CWA relief efforts, the successive federal relief program goals, established through the Works Progress Administration and the National Youth Administration, would have experienced far less initial success. The CWA established a relief network, advocated education and skills training, and attempted to remove the stigma of poverty and relief through the dignity of work. These efforts created bonds of trust between the federal government, state administering agencies, and relief recipients that the WPA and the NYA could build upon. These later agencies went beyond supplying relief and hoped to instill a work ethic and impart some necessary skills to workers ill-equipped to participate in an industrialized and increasingly corporate service economy.

SWEET RELIEF: WOMEN, WORK, AND THE WPA

The great maze of federal programs created between 1933 and 1937 served to allay a considerable assortment of economic ills and human suffering. The FERA and the Public Works Administration (PWA), established in May and June of 1933, provided the first wave of relief. The FERA allocated funding for work and direct relief to state governments; the PWA financed large-scale construction projects and required local government funding participation. FERA work and direct relief programs imposed minimum wage requirements and frequent assessment of need among recipients, so the funding was not entirely unrestricted. With one exception during the winter of 1933-34, when the CWA provided immediate short-term work relief, the FERA and the PWA provided the bulk of direct and work relief until 1935. Nationwide, the FERA proved highly successful in providing immediate relief to the unemployed and the poor. After two years of substantial federal funding, Congress abolished the FERA and replaced it with three agencies—the Resettlement Administration, the National Youth Administration, and the Works Progress Administration—that provided work relief, training, and public works funds and eliminated direct federal relief money.[30]

Of all the federal programs established, the WPA affected the lives of women most profoundly. All classes of laboring women participated in WPA programs. In Georgia, most of the county administrators were women, and despite evidence of gender and racial occupational discrimination in New Deal relief programs, hundreds of women benefited from the WPA.[31] Gay B. Shepperson, federal administrator of Georgia relief programs, explained that "the major objective of the women's work programs of WPA is to provide employment for women breadwinners which would bring them immediate financial assistance."[32]

Shepperson focused her relief organization on the female breadwinner because she recognized the significant role women played in family economies. Early statistical research, commissioned by Shepperson and other relief administrators, indicated that nearly one-fourth of the families on relief rolls had female heads of household. Black women had consistently participated in Atlanta's paid workforce, often as breadwinners, throughout the 1920s. White women, through textile manufacturing employment and white-collar occupations, increased their participation in the city's workforce during and after World War I, but often as supplementary workers. Despite their history of labor force participation, female breadwinners remained on the fringes of the female workforce, especially in prosperous times. But as men began to lose their jobs, female family members and single, widowed, divorced, or separated women fell into the relief spotlight.[33]

Most WPA women's employment projects served the unskilled and endeavored to teach these women domestic skills. The women's service projects, begun under the CWA and expanded after 1935 under the WPA, engaged the largest share of the female unemployed in sewing rooms. More than 1,200 needy women in Fulton and DeKalb counties entered sewing rooms in November 1935. Eight sewing rooms operated in the metropolitan counties by the mid-1930s. Atlanta women composed 8 percent of a total of 34,830 WPA workers in the state by October 1936. The sewing rooms employed most of these women.[34]

Shepperson attempted to provide varied tasks for unemployed women through the WPA, but few relief projects existed for skilled women. Jane Van DeVrede, director of women's service projects in Georgia and a trained nurse who had worked with Shepperson and Harry Hopkins at the Red Cross in New Orleans, lobbied extensively for female professionals, especially nurses. Atlanta professional women, mostly teachers and nurses, represented less than 1 percent of the workers on relief (see Table 6.2). These unemployed professionals administered health education projects and midwife training in rural areas.[35]

Shepperson and VanDeVrede promoted the professional women's projects, especially among Atlanta clubwomen, as a means of social reform and work relief. As public welfare and health professionals, both women believed that skilled workers should administer the work relief programs. One of the first decisions Gay Shepperson made as state director of the FERA eliminated untrained county relief administrators. She filled these positions mostly with female social workers. This decision resulted partly from Governor Eugene Talmage's appointment of political cronies to important county and state administrative positions. Shepperson, originally from Virginia, had spent her career in the social work and welfare profession.[36] Nearly all of the professional projects, except the library projects, employed trained social workers or health professionals and sought to teach rural and unskilled women domestic skills. Dubbed "the home-making program," these efforts initiated by the CWA and later the WPA employed home economists, nurses, hygienists, dietitians, teachers, and librarians to improve the lives of the unskilled and the unemployed. More than one hundred Atlanta clubwomen gathered in December 1933 to show their support for the domestic relief programs.[37]

Although these projects had good intentions, they did not teach most women skills marketable in the private sector. The largest federal programs, especially the sewing projects, employed women in jobs that replicated the nonpaid work they performed in the home and perpetuated the idea that poverty among women could be eradicated through improved domestic skills. As relief rolls began to shrink in 1936, Atlanta WPA administrators felt women returned to their homes "better equipped for the task of thrifty management." Van DeVrede and Shepperson both stated that the CWA and WPA domestic projects emphasized domestic skills so that women forced to seek work relief would not be drafted into an industrial system as permanent wage-labor. This philosophy dovetailed with popular sentiments that viewed women's paid work, and especially married women's work, during the Depression as an attack on out-of-work males.[38]

Although publicly advocating domestic conservatism, both Van DeVrede and Shepperson also supported occupational advancement for white-collar and professional women workers. In their public speaking campaigns, both women stated that women's WPA employment, specifically administrative positions, should not substitute for careers in the private sector. Although many clerical workers were temporary relief recipients, training conferences held in the late 1930s for supervisors and professionals indicated an investment in these women's careers.[39] Politically astute, both Shepperson and Van DeVrede placated critics of women's Depression-era workforce participation by emphasizing the temporary nature of WPA projects.

Clerical work and library projects, the second largest women's employment program after the sewing projects, did not reflect the domestic tenor common among most women's employment under the WPA. These jobs required women to possess specific skills, and the projects rarely served middle-class reformist goals. However, clerical work and library projects proved harder to establish, and fewer women benefited from these programs. Shepperson encountered many difficulties engaging sponsors among local governments, which shouldered some of the costs for professional projects. Material outlays tended to be negligible, but skilled urban wages and administrative costs frequently required a disproportionate share of WPA state allotments, which drew criticism from political opponents of the New Deal. As a result, few professional projects existed, and those located outside larger population centers were hard to initiate.

The library projects proved to be the most successful professional program created by the WPA.[40] This success stemmed from the broad audience that the projects served. Van DeVrede noted that "almost every library worker is a member of some local club or organization and she can bring books to the attention of her fellow club members."[41] In Fulton and DeKalb counties, the WPA library project operated seven public libraries; one in Decatur was also a traveling library, later known as the bookmobile. Throughout the metropolitan area, the WPA assisted twenty-six libraries, most of them located in public schools, including Girls and Boys high schools and the Opportunity School. Local sponsors supported library projects more readily than other professional projects because the program produced tangible results: more books, cheap entertainment, and advanced educational opportunities for children. Even New Deal detractors rarely criticized the library projects.[42]

The library projects, although successful, did not engage many needy women. In May 1934, when all CWA work ended, the WPA reported that professional females composed .08 percent of Atlanta's unemployed female workforce. Of that number, over half (43 out of 70 reporting) were teachers and nurses. Librarians were not counted separately. By March 1935, the state's library projects engaged 93 women in library work, only five of whom were trained librarians.[43]

Contrasted to the specialized work librarians performed, female clerical workers engaged in many phases of WPA and PWA projects. Nearly every construction project required clerical labor, and even the specialized projects within the library program or the health education program utilized clerical labor. Despite the general applicability of clerical skills, early WPA projects frequently placed some trained clerical workers in nonclerical, even unskilled, work relief projects.[44]

Initiating skilled women's work under the WPA proved more complicated than establishing sewing rooms or managing the short-term CWA projects. Through the CWA program, Georgia's 159 counties received clerical assistance from approximately 1,700 white-collar workers. By contrast, the CWA sewing program was huge. It operated 121 sewing rooms that employed more than 4,000 women statewide. When the CWA projects terminated, the sewing rooms transferred easily to the WPA because they employed the unskilled, the majority of the needy, and local administrators could maintain existing projects. The CWA clerical projects did not merge into the WPA projects so easily. Clerical work projects required greater organization at the state and the local level, and frequently county relief administrators could not establish clerical work projects within their local governments. As a result, some women expecting to move from CWA clerical positions to WPA Professional and Women's Projects found themselves unemployed or underemployed. To avoid widespread hardship during the transition, Shepperson placed some former clerical workers in sewing rooms in order to maintain their employment.[45]

Large southern urban areas, like Atlanta, began WPA clerical work projects almost immediately. In March 1935, VanDeVrede reported to Ellen Woodward, Assistant Administrator of Professional and Women's Projects of the WPA in Washington, that Fulton and DeKalb counties employed female clerical workers to index the Decatur water tax records and other property records and provided clerical assistance to the Atlanta City Comptroller. Clerical work projects employed a total of 543 women throughout the state; sewing programs engaged thousands of women. Despite the success of clerical projects in Atlanta, most counties in the state had few clerical work projects. Van DeVrede reported that "most women's work involved sewing."[46]

Atlanta served as both the state headquarters for WPA projects and as the regional center for federal relief operations in the southeast. As a result, most clerical work opportunities directly associated with the administration of WPA programs were located in Atlanta. Nearly all of the statistical survey programs conducted in Georgia and regionwide operated out of Atlanta. Georgia had the second largest area office with fifty-one administrators and support staff. Texas had the largest. Washington field representatives suggested several times that project level clerical work performed in Atlanta should be removed to area offices with smaller administrative staffs where their was a need for skilled relief work.[47]

Shepperson and VanDeVrede felt frustrated at their inability to create more skilled relief work in small towns and rural areas. Inept county administrators, lack of local sponsorship, and limited numbers of needy skilled women workers scuttled attempts to launch significant professional projects in areas outside of Atlanta, Macon, Columbus, or Savannah.

Despite obstacles, the Georgia Professional and Women's Projects expanded greatly throughout the 1930s, reaching a peak of 18,000 female relief recipients working on more than 1,000 projects statewide in 1936.[48] The following year, sewing rooms still employed the bulk of the 10,435 Georgia female work relief recipients, but clerical work projects, despite an overall reduction in relief workforces, showed growth. In November 1937, 90 clerical assistance projects employed 673 men and women in Georgia. By December 1938, the records and statistical surveys projects alone employed 1,272. Clerical assistance projects employed both men and women in Atlanta, frequently in similar proportions. Typically, the most routine clerical tasks such as filing, typing, and indexing public records employed twice as many women as men.[49]

Georgia WPA administrators, especially Van DeVrede and Shepperson, strove to handle relief needs evenhandedly, especially among the various groups of unemployed and needy women. Nevertheless, critics frequently challenged the efficacy of New Deal programs. A particularly vocal critic of the WPA, the Georgia Women's Democratic Club (WDC), wrote several letters in 1937 that accused FERA Director Harry Hopkins of abusing women relief recipients by "dropping" some women workers but not others. WPA policy required that relief workers relinquish their positions after eighteen months and reenter the relief rolls, if necessary, to receive further work relief. County administrators and permanent agency staff were not subject to the same eighteen-month rule. Neither Shepperson nor Van DeVrede indicated in their correspondence that skilled administrators came from relief rolls and often lamented the fact that competent county-level administrators were rare outside the larger Georgia towns and cities. The Georgia WDC, witnessing these apparent inequities, fired off several angry letters to President Roosevelt.

> Why not drop the women with husbands working? I can supply the list, many on [the] administrative payroll, and use WPA for what it was intended for?[50]

Shepperson and VanDeVrede continually battled to employ as many needy women as possible in WPA projects and yet remain true to the spirit of the WPA. Although the Works Progress Administration did not formally change its emphasis to community service projects until after 1939, when it established the Community Services Division, the

WPA between 1935 and 1939 had clearly attempted to provide employment that stimulated the economy, enriched the worker, and served the community. These expansive goals frequently encountered criticism, and public relations for WPA projects assumed a significant part of Shepperson's, and especially Van DeVrede's, time.

Responding to the WDC's criticism of women's work relief policies, Van DeVrede and Shepperson mounted the podium to speak to women's groups, especially the WDC. They addressed social, religious, and professional women's groups throughout the state. The content and tone of these addresses indicate that women's groups frequently failed to recognize the economic realities of family needs and never quite relinquished their belief in the link between morality and poverty. Shepperson noted that female breadwinners composed one-third of women certified for relief in Georgia. She also stressed that creating women's work relief was more difficult than the highly visible male manual work projects. Few unskilled tasks for women existed that contributed in some way to the general welfare of society. VanDeVrede also spoke extensively and frequently employed the radio airwaves to send her message to the Atlanta public. Both women emphasized that women's relief work often fulfilled family needs and attempted to soothe fears that women on relief would replace men in the workforce once the economy improved.

> Recognition of these great family needs makes the providing of jobs
> for women a greater problem than providing work for men, and
> merits the consideration of projects that shall not lose sight of the
> important phase of recovery of normal housework for this great
> number of women who cannot and should not be absorbed in the
> industrial system.[51]

WPA women's projects posed significant problems. Because the majority of the needy were unskilled, "manual" projects benefited the greatest number. However, women's manual projects provided few long-term occupation benefits and had negligible impacts upon the general welfare of nonurban communities. Privately, Shepperson confessed that work relief in nonurban areas did little to alleviate the poverty among the rural poor, which she felt was endemic to the rural South and only exacerbated by the Depression.[52]

Conservatism regarding racial customs and women's participation in paid work created more strife between local WPA project administrators and community groups. Those groups that faulted the New Deal generally found an easy mark for their criticism among the women's projects. Sewing programs, the Georgia WDC claimed, humiliated and embarrassed women because of their sweatshop atmosphere, and in rural areas with limited facilities, the programs frequently trespassed racial customs by allowing black and white women to perform similar work in large shared rooms.[53]

By 1937-1938, when many relief programs stagnated because of upswings in private employment, the Women's and Professional Projects continued to grow. Some New Deal detractors criticized this growth as unnecessary "make-work" that diverted skilled workers from more competitive, and frequently underpaid, private industry positions. The WPA work projects also gained a reputation as dumping grounds for undesirables—those whom private industry would not employ even in times of prosperity, particularly aging workers and unskilled female breadwinners.

Age and gender characteristics among WPA workers differed quite sharply from those in private industry. In Georgia, the professional and service projects employed the largest proportion of women workers among nonconstruction relief projects. White-collar projects in 1938 accounted for 3,763 persons on relief, and 75 percent of these workers were women. In 1940, private industry employed relatively even proportions of men and women in clerical and sales occupations. VanDeVrede pointed out that the median age of WPA workers was considerably higher than in private industry and should serve as an example that older workers were capable of remaining in the workforce.[54]

TWENTY YEARS LATER

After two decades, the characteristics of female clerical workers had changed dramatically. Race remained the only constant factor in female clerical employment. In 1940, 14,684 Atlanta women had office occupations, and nearly 98 percent were white. Because this overwhelmingly white occupation experienced consistent growth, the rate of workforce participation among white women rose dramatically. By 1940, 26 percent of Atlanta's employed residents and 30 percent of its employed women held office work positions. Domestic service employment among black women, which had reached its zenith during

**Table 6.3: Atlanta Females Employed & Seeking Work
Selected Occupations, 1940**

White Occupations	Total	Employed	Percent	Seeking Work	Percent
Professional & Semiprofessionals	4346	4216	97	130	3
Clerical	15429	14684	95	745	5
Operatives	7516	6755	90	761	10
Service	6379	5830	91	549	9
Black Occupations					
Domestic Service	17030	15248	89.5	1782	10.5

Source: U.S. Department of Commerce, *Sixteenth Census, Population*, "Occupations," 1940.

Table 6.4: Clerical Workers and Marital Status, 1920 & 1940

	Total Clerical	No. Single	Percent	No. Married	Percent
1920	6,112	4,360	71	1023	16
1940	28,559	15,135	53	10,470	37

Source: U.S. Department of Commerce, *Fourteenth Census, Population,*
"Occupations," and *Sixteenth Census, Population,* "Occupations."

the post-World War I period, had declined from nearly 75 percent of employed females to 31 percent. Increasingly, white women seeking work in Atlanta throughout the 1930s tread a well-worn path into the downtown business district.

These women were older and more of them were married than their counterparts in the immediate postwar years. In 1920, single women held 71 percent of the city's office positions, and married women accounted for 16 percent. By 1940, single women still held 53 percent of the clerical positions, but married women had doubled their clerical workforce participation to 37 percent.[55] Despite the halting economic recovery, persistent criticism of married women workers, and a large pool of young, single women to draw from, Atlanta employers retained older and married women workers. The philosophy of expendable female office labor, characteristic of 1920s female clerical employment, subsided during the Depression. The Retail Credit Company, which had greatly enlarged its female clerical workforce during the 1920s, suspended hiring nonessential personnel until the worst of the crisis had passed. Company managers felt compelled to retain experienced personnel because training programs for new employees had been trimmed. However, the company still required married women to resign.

For many working women the Depression era represented a period of stagnation and even decline in occupational opportunities, salaries, and professional growth. In 1934, sociologist Lorine Pruette studied the members of the American Women's Association in New York City, a white-collar, urban women's professional organization. The "typical AWA member," she wrote, is past forty, unmarried with an education, experienced in the workforce, and sustains a high cost of living. Among these women, the Depression instilled a great fear of joblessness and a willingness to demand less in terms of professional and occupational growth. They also tolerated undesirable circumstances longer than they would have in the prosperous 1920s. For those single women who prevailed over joblessness, the solidarity of other women contributed significant moral, if not financial, support.[56]

Before the Depression, female clerical workers frequently changed jobs, often in search of better opportunities and wages. Confidence in their abilities and some form of safety net—savings, skills, or family— allowed some women to continue to seek out better opportunities. But for women like Stella Brady, keeping a job was more important than getting a better job. In the mid-1940s, widowed and on her own, Stella stayed on at her job even though she felt underpaid and undervalued. "They all were making better money than I was," she reflected on fellow Business and Professional Women's Club members. "I would hear them talk." In retrospect, Stella felt some resentment. "Just when they knew I was going to leave, [the PTA] raised my salary. You know, they didn't appreciate me."[57]

NOTES

1. Douglas Fleming, "Atlanta, the Depression, and the New Deal" (Ph. D. diss., Emory University, 1984), 64-67.

2. Rich's sales in 1930 were $342,806 and by 1933 they had dropped to $185,851. Richard Rich adopted innovative retail methods such as the bargain basement, where less-expensive goods could be purchased, and a generous return policy during the Depression that generated intense customer loyalty and catered to working women. Fleming, 67-70.

3. Fleming, 70.

4. False optimism was not an original tactic conceived by Atlanta businessmen. President Herbert Hoover spearheaded the effort to inspire the American people with confidence in the economy through business optimism. Atlanta businessmen followed the advice of Washington and maintained rhetorical optimism although their economic conservatism required that they limit any investments and reduce their workforces. See Robert S. McElvaine, *The Great Depression: America, 1929-1941* (New York: Times Books, 1984), 72-94, passim.

5. Douglas L. Smith, *The New Deal and the Urban South* (Baton Rouge: Louisiana State University Press, 1988), 63.

6. In 1930, sociologist Arthur L. Raper, then a professor at Agnes Scott College in Decatur, stated that "from Greene County [east of Atlanta] alone some 30,000 colored people have come into Atlanta." Fleming, 70.

7. Fleming, 32-33, 37; William C. Holley, Ellen Winston, and T. J. Woofter, Jr., *The Plantation South, 1934-1937*, WPA Research Monograph XXII (Washington, D.C.: GPO, 1940; repr., New York: Da Capo Press, 1971), 48-49. Population trends in the early 1930s showed that southern farm families furnished more than one-fourth of the total increase in the nation's labor supply in the 1930s. They shifted their labor from agricultural pursuits to towns and villages where the increased labor supply could not be absorbed.

8. Fleming, 99-100.

9. Progressive reforms sprung from the moral-laden middle class which penned such phrases as the "deserving poor." Governor Eugene Talmage, hostile to federal "interference" in state relief efforts and aid to the unemployed, suggested that the needy would return to work if authorities would "line them up against the wall and give them castor oil." Michael S. Holmes, *The New Deal in Georgia: An Administrative History* (Westport, Connecticut: Greenwood Press, 1975), 28.

10. Evangelical Ministers Association Minutes, 7 September 1931, Atlanta History Center.

11. Fleming, 109-110.

12. Smith, 37-38.

13. U. S. Department of Commerce, Bureau of the Census, *Fifteenth Census of the United States, 1930, Population*, "Occupations," 378-382. Katherine D. Wood, "Urban Workers on Relief: Part II, The Occupational Characteristics of Workers on Relief in 79 Cities, May 1934," *Research Monograph IV* (Washington: GPO, 1937):92-93, 110-111, 118-119.

14. Wandersee, 1-54 passim. Wandersee posits that increased consumption and the large-scale transition to a money economy for many American families created a new definition of economic need during the 1920s and the 1930s. Economic need throughout the Depression varied greatly among urban and rural dwellers and middle-class and working-class families.

15. Faith M. Williams and Alice C. Hanson, "Expenditure Habits of Wage Earners and Clerical Workers" *Monthly Labor Review* 49 (December 1939): 1311-1334, passim.

16. Stella Brady, interview by author, Tape recording, 21 April 1987 and Marie Cooper, interview by author, Tape recording, 5 August 1989.

17. Faith M. Williams, "Money Disbursements of Wage Earners and Clerical Workers in Richmond, Birmingham, and New Orleans" *Monthly Labor Review* 42 (May 1936): 1460.

18. Fleming, 77.

19. "Influence of Depression on Expenditures of Business Women," *Monthly Labor Review* 27 (December 1933), 1359-1360; in the fall of 1931, the

YWCA requested that their members, primarily in clerical occupations, keep detailed records of their spending habits. Data was collected from 313 women and girls in 1931, and 147 of the 313 also reported spending figures for fall 1932. The study revealed that out of 128 women reporting for both years, 65 percent were receiving lower wages in 1932 than in 1931. Of those receiving wage cuts, the lowest income group experienced the most cuts. The Bureau of Labor Statistics grieved that "the insecurity of the low-wage group is again borne witness to."

20. Julia Kirk Blackwelder, "Letters from the Great Depression: A Tour Through A Collection of Letters To An Atlanta Newspaperwomen," *Southern Exposure* 6 (1978): 74.

21. *City Builder* 16 (February 1932): 11.

22. "Relief Roster in Atlanta Analyzed by Occupations," Atlanta *Constitution*, 24 April 1935, 9. The *Constitution* reported that "Of the major group of 11,000 domestic and personal service workers on relief 94 percent were negroes. More than half, or 6,200 had formerly been employed as household servants."

23. Smith, 68.

24. As might be expected, race significantly affected which teachers would be unemployed. The *Constitution* reported that: "Professionals represented only 1 percent of the workers on relief in Atlanta during May. Most numerous were school teachers, of whom nearly 200 were on the rolls, including 150 negro teachers." "Relief Roster . . .," *Constitution* 24 April 1935, 9.

25. Fleming, 47-50, 80; Smith, 33, 37-38.

26. Holmes, 19-33, passim, a thorough account of the Talmage-Hopkins-Shepperson struggle; Smith, 72; Fleming, 143-44. *Constitution*, 6 January 1934, 1 and 10 January 1934, 10. Most of Talmage's appointees had no experience with relief administration or public welfare policy. Shepperson, appointed director of federal relief programs in Georgia over Talmage's objections, engaged in numerous acrimonious battles with Talmage throughout the early years of the federal program. FERA director Harry Hopkins appointed Shepperson state director because Talmage, like several southern governors, could not separate political patronage from relief.

27. Fleming, 143; Smith, 66.

28. A Transient Bureau, established in October 1933, processed many migrants in five Georgia cities: Atlanta, Macon, Savannah, Augusta, and Columbus. In January 1934, Florida banned transients from relief programs and further swelled the number of migrants in Georgia. "Georgia to Open Five Bureaus to Aid Transient Unemployed," Atlanta *Constitution* 11 October 1933: 1; Smith, 72-73; Fleming, 145, 153.

29. Ecke, 242; Fleming, 116-17; Smith, 69.

30. Holmes, 87.

31. Blackwelder, *Caste and Class*, 118-120. Blackwelder notes that despite the establishment of women's divisions and service projects and the prominence of women in New Deal agencies, the female unemployed were treated as second-class citizens. Job preference was given to male heads or separated or widowed female heads of households. Racial social customs also prejudiced some administrators' views on relief programs. Jane Van DeVrede, Director of Women's Service Projects in Georgia under the CWA and the WPA, seemed perplexed when former black domestic workers failed to show enthusiasm for domestic training projects supervised by the "southern gentle woman, last survivors of the old aristocracy" chosen by Van DeVrede; Holmes, 80.

32. Gay B. Shepperson made no apologies for her attempts to provide relief to female breadwinners, many of whom were likely widowed or separated. See "1,438 Have Left Rolls To Accept Better Paying Positions in Private Employment During Year," Atlanta *Constitution* 1 November 1936, sec. K, 7.

33. Kessler-Harris, *Out to Work*, Chapter 9 "Some Benefits of Labor Segregation in a Decade of Depression", passim.

34. "Varied WPA Tasks Provided for Women," Atlanta *Constitution* 15 November 1936, sec. A, 11.

35. Script of WSB Broadcast, "Recreation Project Program" by Van DeVrede, 15 May 1937, TMs, Van DeVrede Collection, Georgia Department of Archives and History, Atlanta.

36. Holmes, 25-28.

37. Speech by Van DeVrede to the Democratic Women's Club Convention in Valdosta, Georgia 17 November 1938, TMs, Van DeVrede Collection, Georgia Department of Archives and History; "Georgia Women Pledge Volunteer Service to Promote CWA" Atlanta *Constitution* 13 December 1933, 14.

38. Fred Denton Moon, "How the CWA Aids Women" *Atlanta Journal Magazine* 21 January 1934, 3; "Atlanta Women Pledge Volunteer Service to Promote CWA," Atlanta *Constitution* 13 December 1933, 14; Atlanta *Constitution* 1 November 1936, sec. K, 7; Kessler-Harris, 250-252.

39. Text of speech by Van DeVrede to Democratic Women's Club of Valdosta, 17 November 1938, Van DeVrede Collection, Georgia Department of Archives and History. Van DeVrede emphasized the large turnover in WPA programs, which she felt indicated that women did not make careers of WPA work. However, at a training conference for Area and Assistant Area

Supervisors of the Women's and Professional Projects held in Atlanta in December 1938, discussions focused on how administrative employees would be integrated into civil service. Clearly, the WPA programs would not provide careers of great longevity for professionals and supervisors, but many of these women maintained WPA employment for periods of several years or more.

40. Professional programs covered a broad range of skills and training. Many of the clerical and library works projects employed educated unemployed women in routine tasks such as filing, bookbinding, and book repair. Other jobs required occupational skills including: typing, stenography, library science, and management. Some training occurred, especially for the unskilled. Clerical work projects taught rudimentary office skills, such as filing and answering phones, as well as office etiquette. The library projects also concentrated most training on rudimentary skills.

41. "December Training Institute for WPA Library Clerks," Van DeVrede Collection, Georgia Department of Archives and History.

42. "Professional and Service Projects in Fulton and DeKalb Counties" n.d., TMs, Government Documents, Emory University, Atlanta.

43. WPA files (Record Group 69, National Archives) are organized by agency and state. The Georgia state files contain summaries of state projects, but rarely contained information on projects at the county or municipal level. Presumably, county administrators submitted reports to state administrators who reported to Washington, DC. Therefore, all figures associated with WPA projects for professional and women's projects are based on statewide totals.

44. "Summary of Relief Activities in Georgia," report by Shepperson to Federal Agencies Conference, 10 April 1936, Atlanta, Van DeVrede Collection.

45. "A History of the Georgia Civil Works Administration 1933-1934, by Miss Jane Van DeVrede prepared under the supervision of Miss Gay B. Shepperson, Administrator," TMs, Jane Van DeVrede Collection, Georgia State Department of Archives and History, Atlanta. H. Reid Hunter, Superintendent of Schools to Miss Gay B. Shepperson, TL, 20 April 1934, Van DeVrede Collection.

46. Gay B. Shepperson to Ellen Woodward, TL, 21 March 1935, RG 69, Records of the Works Progress Administration, State Files (Georgia), Box 1156, File No. 661, National Archives.

47. Georgia Field Representative (name unknown) to Malcom Miller, file copy of Memo on field trip conducted April 22-26, 1938, RG 69, State Files WPA.

48. Van DeVrede WSB broadcast, 15 May 1937.

49. Memo from Mrs. Cole to Miss Woodward, 24 November 1937, RG 69, State Files, Box 1159; "Georgia Project Status Report, October 31, 1937," RG 69, State Files, Box 583; Memo to File from Malcom Miller, Field Representative, Georgia Field Trip April 22-26, 1938, RG 69, State Files, Box 584.

50. Mrs. Estelle Wellington Stevenson, President, Georgia Women's Democratic Club, to President Roosevelt, 26 July 1937, RG 69, Box 1144.

51. Script of WSB broadcast delivered by Jane Van DeVrede, 15 May 1937, Van DeVrede Collection.

52. Holmes, 88.

53. Homes, 132.

54. Text of speech to the Democratic Women's Club Convention by Van DeVrede, November 17, 1938, Van DeVrede Collection.

55. In 1920, approximately 13 percent of the female clerical workforce was divorced, widowed, or separated. In 1940, only 10 percent of the same workforce identified themselves as widowed, divorced, or separated.

56. Pruette, *Women Workers Through the Depression*, 47-48.

57. Stella Brady, interview with author.

Conclusion

One of the questions that impelled this work asked if differences existed between the experiences of southern female office workers and those of other urban female office workers. Numerous studies have examined the work lives and political and social environments of female clerical workers in Chicago, Pittsburgh, Albany, and in the nation. The hierarchical structure of offices, the feminization of the workforce—specifically low-level positions—pay scales, hours, environments, opportunity, and even social organizations among business women in each of these cities all resemble one another. Each city established educational programs to train office workers. Employers across the country scrambled to hire young girls fresh from high school. And many women expressed optimism about clerical work opportunities.

Yet, most women worked within offices characterized by patriarchal and paternalistic corporate authority that significantly limited occupational opportunity. These environments had been established before women entered office positions in significant numbers, but they were especially effective upon young, single, female workers who had rarely been independent of family, religious, or educational authority and whose labor experience was limited. For thousands of Atlanta women, office work presented a conundrum. It offered some measure of independence, but also often limited aspirations because careers or livelihoods were preempted by marriage, and gender boundaries were imposed by employers and condoned by religious and social organizations. The twentieth-century commercial city bound its most modern symbol, the female office worker, to the previous century's social codes. Despite their vital role in the process of urbanization, Atlanta's female office workers did not significantly profit from the city's commercial expansion in their work or social lives.

These women rarely vocalized their discontent. Few women wanted to discuss their work for use in this study. When they spoke of ill feelings toward former bosses, or the inadequacy of their wages, they often regretted the remarks as though they feared some reprisals. Few of these women had pensions that could be jeopardized. Yet, they did not want to appear ungrateful. Most of the women interviewed had great fondness for their work, appreciated their skills, and found pleasure in working, but every one had at least one story that indicated how the mix of business and morality adversely affected their work and limited their social endeavors.

The Atlanta business community responded to requests to view company records with similar reluctance. Most business histories of Atlanta firms do not focus on personnel issues or the tenor of employee and management interactions. The Equifax company generously allowed use of their library, publications, and historical memorabilia, but several attempts to interview female employees drew negative responses. A company-sponsored historian had similar experiences with the peer group I sought to interview. This reluctance to share information or speak openly about work and a work group vital to the city's growth is frustrating to the scholar. It indicates how deeply the control, exercised by male corporate authority figures upon their female workforces and condoned by social and civic bodies, imbedded itself in the city's female office workforce. To this day, little labor consciousness exists among southern office workforces, which are mostly female. In the 1920s and the 1930s, none existed other than a vague aspiration to succeed at respectable and often well-paid employment.

Women's frustration at the limitations of clerical work was not openly expressed in corporate work environments. Paternalism can explain some of this reluctance. Although hard to prove, paternalistic authority models created employee and supervisor relationships that seemed generous but frequently imposed unfair restrictions that could not be openly questioned. Hidden behind a patronizing, persuasive, and even logical voice, paternalism applied to intensely personal arenas, such as marriage or family morality, and implied that noncompliance would threaten one's job. It thrived in a system that pit the individual against her peer, but that invited the individual to seek confidences in the company, supervisor, or iconographic authority figure. The goodness of the individual became the watermark whereby corporations measured their workforce and their corporate identity.

Most southern historians who describe regional distinctiveness delve into the concept of paternalism. Broadly, paternalism is an enigmatic function of hegemony that applies to many social relations including racial polemics, gender relations, and class structure. Within the corporate environment, paternalism was not distinctive or at least rarely as blatant as it was in Piedmont textile towns or in the dynamics of Jim Crow race relations. Businesses established distinctions between men and women within the office and summoned social mores to justify these distinctions. These criteria often had nothing to do with work-related skills, but were clearly gender-biased. Or at least it is clear now that bias existed. Businesses hired women into office positions based on an array of nonwork related qualifications. Marital status, home life, fidelity to previous employers, age, appearance, and social affiliations became qualifiers for female office work employment, as much as skills, experience, and ability were. Once a woman secured a position, her work performance competed against her marital status and age and played a significant part in the decision to keep her employed or allow her to rise to her ambitions. Lisa Fine writes that for many women these qualifiers, in addition to the stagnancy of clerical work positions, trampled women's hopes.

Atlanta employers operated from positions of strength. Applauded by the city's leaders, businessmen used their elevated social and political status to mold a workforce that suited their needs. They also influenced the social organizations linked to this workforce. Employers emphasized character qualifications and established familial authority hierarchies within offices that their predominantly middle-class female workforce found familiar. Large businesses relied heavily on clannish loyalty to personalized corporate ideals, company mottoes, and management/employee camaraderie to prevent the degradation of their clerical workforces into bored automatons. Some employers did not earn the loyalty or respect of their female employees or the women did not validate their attempts to foster loyalty. Women frequently changed jobs to gain better positions, and employers with small workforces and low salaries probably sought warm bodies rather than skilled or loyal workers.

When women sought appreciation, they often looked within their church and female associations. Atlanta's business women's organizations are important to understanding the commercial climate of the city as white-collar women perceived it. These groups do not evoke women's lives as fully as their family experiences, domestic responsibilities, or their demographics might. However, as working women's social and political representatives, they indicate loyalties, choices, and aspirations.

Atlanta's traditional women's network emerged in the late nineteenth century and served educated elite women who sought intellectual companionship, performed religious and civic welfare work, or met for social purposes. World War I changed women's organizations and energized a group of women that had organized but had not established an agenda. These business women's groups, similar to their predecessors, met primarily for social stimulation and endeavored to contribute to civic improvement. With the increase of white-collar businesswomen in the city and the nation during the 1920s, some businesswomen's organizations evolved from social peer clubs to self-gratifying, socially conscious, working women's advocates. Few of these clubs favored political activism. The women did not declare themselves feminists, as they defined feminism. But their perceptions of themselves as women and as citizens broadened significantly and laid the groundwork for later female public involvement in politics, the arts, and as city builders.

Individual female clerical workers entered business women's clubs for association. Many clubs sponsored social activities and enjoined women who labored together to fraternize outside the confines of the office. Relationships within the office seemed rare, especially among women who had to commute. Many women did not belong to businesswomen's clubs, but they chose to organize in churches, through women's auxiliaries, or sororities. These women chose different affiliations—spiritual, intellectual, or social—but they almost always chose to identify themselves as businesswomen. It was a badge they wore proudly.

The Depression acted as an erosive force upon the gains businesswomen had accumulated. Wages decreased, sexual work discrimination spread rapidly, especially with the ignominious approval of the U.S. Congress, and many women's right to work became suspect in the face of massive unemployment. For women who had steadily watched the growth and acceptance of female white-collar employment during the 1920s, the decade that followed must have disappointed them. When defense employment soared—female clerical workers entered Army bases and Washington DC throughout 1940 and 1941 in anticipation of military intervention—women from all employment sectors greeted these opportunities gladly. Stenographers and typists in Atlanta were trained at the Opportunity School, fully paid, in preparation for War Department jobs. Their World War II work experiences altered women's clerical work opportunities in ways that are reminiscent of women's World War I work involvement. The late 1940s and 1950s, like the 1920s and 1930s, ushered in a distinct era of women's work history.

Sources

ARCHIVAL MATERIAL

Emory University, Special Collections, Woodruff Library, Atlanta

Mary Cornelia Barker Collection, Southern Summer School for
    Workers
Maybelle Jones Dewey Papers
Charles Palmer Papers
Medora Field Perkerson Papers
Richard Rich Papers
Mildred Seydell Papers
Young Women's Christian Association Collection

Department of Archives and History, State of Georgia, Atlanta

Jane Van DeVrede Collection, WPA Records and Other Papers, 1913–
    1973,
Business and Professional Women's Club of Atlanta, Uncatalogued
Georgia Power Collection
Creighton Business College

Atlanta History Center, Library and Archives

Central Presbyterian Church
Evangelical Ministers Association, Christian Council of Atlanta (Men
    and Religion Forward Movement)
Samuel W. and Elizabeth Hanleiter McCallie Papers
Girls' High School Collection, 1937–1961

Pilot Club Collection
Second Ponce de Leon Baptist Church
Southern Women's Educational Alliance, Subject File
Atlanta Women's Chamber of Commerce
Atlanta Women's Club
Gay B. Shepperson Papers

Equifax, Corporate Headquarters, Atlanta, Georgia

Retail Credit Company Records, 1916–1940

National Archives, Washington, D.C.

Works Projects Administration, General Files and State Files, Georgia,
   Record Group 69

NEWSPAPERS AND PERIODICALS

Atlanta Journal Sunday Magazine
Atlanta Constitution
City Builder
Monthly Labor Review

UNPUBLISHED PERIODICAL LITERATURE

Flashlights, Atlanta Business and Professional Women's Club
Inspection Service Journal, Inspection News, and *The Roundtable,*
Retail Credit Company

GOVERNMENT PUBLICATIONS

Harriet A. Byrne. "Women Who Work in Offices," *Women's Bureau
Bulletin 132.* Washington, D.C.: GPO, 1935.
Ethel Erickson. "The Employment of Women in Offices," *Women's
Bureau Bulletin 120.* Washington, D.C.: GPO, 1934.
William C. Holley, Ellen Winston, and T.J. Woofter, Jr., "The
Plantation South, 1934–1937," *Works Progress Administration
Research Monograph XXII.* Washington, D.C.: GPO, 1940.
Amy G. Maher, "Bookkeepers, Stenographers and Office Clerks in
Ohio, 1914 to 1929," *Women's Bureau Bulletin 95.* Washington, D.C.:
GPO, 1932.

Women's Bureau. "Office Work in Houston, 1940" and "Office Work in Richmond, 1940," *Women's Bureau Bulletin 188*. Washington, D.C.: GPO, 1942.

Katherine Wood. "Urban Workers on Relief, May 1934," *Works Progress Administration Research Monograph 4, Part II*. Washington, D.C.: GPO, 1934.

Works Progress Administration. *A Survey of Transient and Homeless Population in Twelve Cities, September 1935 to September 1936*. Washington, D.C.: GPO, 1937.

Works Projects Administration. Professional and Service Projects in Fulton and DeKalb Counties.

SECONDARY WORKS

Allen, Ruth Alice. *The Labor of Women in the Production of Cotton*. Austin, 1930; rpt., New York: Arno Press, 1975.

Aronowitz, Stanley. *False Promises: The Shaping of American Working Class Consciousness*. New York: McGraw-Hill Book Company, 1973.

Anderson, Gregory. *Victorian Clerks*. Manchester: Manchester University Press, 1976.

Aron, Cindy Sondik. *Ladies and Gentlemen of the Civil Service: Middle Class Workers in Victorian America*. New York: Oxford University Press, 1987.

Baker, Elizabeth Faulkner. *Technology and Woman's Work*. New York: Columbia University Press, 1964.

Beard, Mary. *Women's Work in Municipalities*. Arno Press, rpt 1915; National Municipal League Monograph Series.

Blackwelder, Julia Kirk. *Women of the Depression: Caste and Culture in San Antonio, 1929–1939*. College Station, Texas: Texas A & M University, 1984.

Braverman, Harry. *Labor and Monopoly Capital: The Degradation of Work in the Twentieth Century*. New York: Monthly Review Press, 1974.

Breckinridge, Sophinisba P. *Women in the Twentieth Century*. New York: McGraw- Hill, 1933.

Brown, Dorothy. *Setting a Course: American Women in the 1920s*. Boston: Twayne Publishers, 1987.

Callow, Alexander B. Jr., Ed. *American Urban History*. Second Edition. New York: Oxford University Press, 1973.

Carlton, David. *Mill and Town in South Carolina, 1880–1920*. Baton Rouge: Louisiana State University Press, 1982.

Chafe, William H. *Women and Equality: Changing Patterns in American Culture*. Oxford: Oxford University Press, 1977.

Chandler, Alfred, Jr. *The Visible Hand: The Managerial Revolution in American Business*. Cambridge: Harvard University Press, 1977.

Cobb, James. *The Selling of the South: The Southern Crusade for Industrial Development, 1936–1980*. Baton Rouge: Louisiana State University Press, 1982.

Current, Richard N. *The Typewriter and the Men Who Made It*. Urbana: University of Illinois Press, 1954.

Davies, Margery. *Women's Place is at the Typewriter*. Philadelphia: Temple University Press, 1982.

Dillman, Caroline M. Ed. *Southern Women*. New York: Hemisphere Publishing Corporation, 1988.

Dubovsky, Melvin and Stephen Burwood, eds. *Women and Minorities During the Great Depression*. New York: Garland Publishing, 1990.

Ecke, Melvin W. *From Ivy Street to Kennedy Center: Centennial History of the Atlanta Public School System*. Atlanta Board of Education, 1972.

Emmet, Boris and John Jeuck. *Catalogues and Counters: A History of Sears, Roebuck and Company*. Chicago: 1950.

Gamble, Richard H. *A History of the Federal Reserve Bank of Atlanta, 1914–1989*. Federal Reserve Bank of Atlanta, 1989.

Garrett, Franklin M. *Atlanta and Environs*. Vol II. New York: Lewis Publishing Company, 1954.

Gordon, David, Richard Edwards, and Michael Reich. *Segmented Work, Divided Workers: The Historical Transformation of Labor in the U.S.*. Cambridge: Cambridge University Press, 1982.

Gordon, Michael, Ed. *The American Family in Social-Historical Perspective*. Third Edition. New York: St. Martin's Press, 1983.

Greenwald, Maurine W. *Women, War, and Work: The Impact of World War I on Women Workers in the United States*. Westport, Conn.: Greenwood Press, 1980.

Hall, Jacquelyn Dowd. *Revolt Against Chivalry*. New York: Columbia University Press, 1979.

Haygood, Margaret. *Mothers of the South*. Chapel Hill: University of North Carolina Press, 1939; rpt., W.W. Norton, 1977.

Henderson, Alexa Benson. *Atlanta Life Insurance Company: Guardian of Black Economic Dignity.* Tuscaloosa: University of Alabama Press, 1990.

Hill, Samuel, Ed. *Religion and the Old South.* Nashville, Tenn.: Abingdon Press, 1972.

Holmes, Michael. *The New Deal in Georgia: An Administrative History.* Westport, Conn.: Greenwood Press, 1975.

Howe, Louise. *Pink Collar Workers.* New York: Putnam Books, 1977.

Hutchins, Grace. *Women Who Work.* New York: International Publishers, 1934.

Janiewski, Dolores. *Sisterhood Denied: Race, Gender, and Class in a New South Community.* Philadelphia: Temple University Press, 1985.

Jones, Anne Goodwyn. *Tommorrow Is Another Day: The Woman Writer in the South, 1859–1936.* Baton Rouge: Louisiana State University Press, 1981.

Kanter, Rosabeth M. *Men and Women of the Corporation.* New York: Basic Books, 1977.

Katzman, David A. *Seven Days a Week: Women and Domestic Service in Industrializing America.* New York: Oxford University Press, 1978.

Kessler-Harris, Alice. *Out to Work: A History of Wage Earning Women in the U.S.* Oxford: Oxford University Press, 1982.

Kornbluh, Joyce and Mary Frederickson, eds. *Sisterhood and Solidarity: Workers Education for Women, 1914–1984.* Philadelphia: Temple University Press, 1984.

Kraditor, Aileen S. *The Ideas of the Woman Suffrage Movement, 1890–1920.* New York: W.W. Norton & Company, 1981.

Kuhn, Clifford M., Harlon E. Joye, and E. Bernard West. *Living Atlanta: An Oral History of the City, 1914–1948.* Athens: University of Georgia Press, 1990.

Lockwood, David. *The Black-coated Worker: A Study of Class Consciousness.* London: Ruskin House, 1958.

McElvaine, Robert S. *The Great Depression: America, 1929–1941.* New York: Times Books, 1984.

McLaurin, Melton Alonza. *Paternalism and Protest: Southern Cotton Mill Workers and Organized Labor, 1875–1905.* Westport, Conn.: Greenwood Press, 1971.

McMahan, C.A. *The People of Atlanta: A Demographic Study of Georgia's Capital City.* Athens: University of Georgia Press, 1950.

McNally, Fiona. *Women for Hire: A Study of the Female Office Worker*. New York: St. Martin's Press, 1979.

Mills, C. Wright. *White Collar: The American Middle Classes*. New York: Oxford University Press, 1951.

Noble, David. *America By Design: Science, Technology, and the Rise of Corporate Capitalism*. New York: Knopf, 1977.

Pruette, Lorine, ed. *Women Workers through the Depression: A Study of White Collar Employment Made by the American Women's Association*. New York: Macmillan, 1934.

Rotella, Elyce. *From Home to Office: United States Women at Work, 1870–1930*. Ann Arbor: UMI Research Press, 1981.

Rothman, Sheila M. *Woman's Proper Place: A History of Changing Ideals and Practices, 1870 to the Present*. New York: Basic Books, 1978.

Rouse, Jacqueline. *Lugenia Burns Hope, Black Southern Reformer*. Athens: University of Georgia Press, 1989.

Russell, James M. *Atlanta, 1847–1890: City Building in the Old South and the New*. Baton Rouge: Louisiana State University Press, 1988.

Scharf, Lois. *To Work and to Wed: Female Employment, Feminism, and the Great Depression*. Westport, Conn.: Greenwood, 1980.

Scott, Anne Firor. *The Southern Lady: From Pedestal to Politics, 1830–1930*. Chicago: The University of Chicago Press, 1970.

———. *Making the Invisible Woman Visible*. Urbana: University of Illinois Press, 1984.

Smith, Douglas. *The New Deal in the Urban South*. Baton Rouge: Louisiana State University, Press 1988.

Tindall, George. *The Emergence of the New South*, 1913–1945. Baton Rouge: Louisiana State University Press, 1967.

Thomas, Mary. *Riveting and Rationing in Dixie*. Tuscaloosa: University of Alabama Press, 1987.

Wandersee, Winifred D. *Women's Work and Family Values, 1920–1940*. Cambridge: Harvard University Press, 1981.

Ware, Susan. *Holding Their Own: American Women in the 1930s*. Boston: Twayne Publishers, 1982.

Wertheimer, Barbara M. *We Were There: The Story of Working Women in America*. New York: Praeger Publishers, 1983.

Westin, Jeanne. *Making Do: How Women Survived in the '30s*. Chicago: Follett, 1976.

Woodward, C. Van. *Origins of the New South, 1877–1913*. Baton Rouge: Louisiana State University Press, 1967.

Wright, Barbara D. and Myra M Ferree, et.al., eds. *Women, Work, and Technology: Transformation*. Ann Arbor: University of Michigan Press, 1987.

Wright, Gavin. *Old South, New South*. New York: Basic Books, 1986.

Wright, Wade H. *History of the Georgia Power Company, 1855–1956*. Atlanta: Georgia Power Company, 1957.

Dissertations and Theses

Anderson, Mary Christine. "Gender, Class, and Culture: Women Secretarial and Clerical Workers in the U.S., 1925–1955, vols. I & II." Ph.D. diss., Ohio State University, 1986.

Branch, Anne Lavinia. "Atlanta and the American Settlement House Movement." Masters thesis, Emory University, 1966.

Brownell, Blaine. "The Urban Mind of the South: The Growth of Urban Consciousness, 1920–1927." Ph. D. diss., University of North Carolina, Chapel Hill, 1969.

Cohen, Miriam. "From Workshop to Office: Italian Women and Family Strategies in New York City, 1900–1950." Ph.D. diss., University of Michigan, 1978.

Corley, Florence Fleming. "Higher Education for Southern Women: Four Church Related Women's Colleges in Georgia, Agnes Scott, Shorter, Spelman, and Weslyan, 1900–1920." Ph.D. diss., Georgia State University, 1985.

Crimmins, Timothy J. "The Crystal Stair: A Study of the Effects of Class, Race and Ethnicity on Secondary Education in Atlanta, 1872–1925." Ph.D. diss., Emory University, 1972.

Deaton, Thomas. "Atlanta During the Progressive Era." Ph.D. diss., University of Georgia, 1969.

DeVault, Ileen A. "Sons and Daughters of Labor: Class and Clerical Work in Pittsburgh, 1870s-1910s." Ph.D. diss., Yale University, 1985.

Durham, Myrtle Belle. "History of the Atlanta Opportunity School." Masters Thesis, Emory University, 1938.

Fine, Lisa Michelle. "'The Record Keepers of Property': The Making of the Female Labor Force in Chicago, 1870–1930." Ph.D. diss., University of Wisconsin-Madison, 1985.

Fleming, Douglas. "Atlanta, the Depression and the New Deal." Ph.D. diss., Emory University, 1972.

Flinn, William Adams. "A History of Retail Credit Company: A Study in the Marketing of Information About Individuals." Ph.D. diss., Ohio State University, 1959.

Garofalo, Charles. "Business Ideas in Atlanta, 1916–1935." Ph.D. diss., Emory University, 1952.

Henderson, Alexa. "A Twentieth Century Black Enterprise: The Atlanta Life Insurance Company, 1905–1975." Ph.D. diss., Georgia State University, 1975.

Hopkins, Richard. "Patterns of Persistence and Occupational Mobility in a Southern City: Atlanta, 1870–1920." Ph.D. diss., Emory University, 1972.

Hunter, Henry. "The Development of Public Secondary Schools of Atlanta, Georgia." Ph.D. diss., George Peabody College for Teachers, 1938.

Klopper, Ruth. "The Family's Use of Urban Space: Elements of Family Structure and Function Among Economic Elites, Atlanta, Georgia, 1880–1920." Ph.D. diss., Emory University, 1977.

Lovern, Henry M. "Factors Affecting the Employment of Beginning Office Workers in Atlanta, Georgia." Ph.D. diss., Ohio State University, 1967.

McElheny, Mrs. C. J. "The History of Commercial High School and Its Significance." Masters thesis, Ogelthorpe University, 1935.

Nelson, Susan McGrath. "Association of Southern Women for the Prevention of Lynching and the Fellowship of the Concerned: Southern Church Women and Radical Politics." Masters thesis, Emory University, 1982.

Preston, Howard. "A New Kind of Horizontal City: Automobility in Atlanta, 1900– 1930." Ph.D. diss., Emory University, 1974.

Racine, Philip. "Atlanta's Public Schools: A History of the Public School System, 1869–1965." Ph.D. diss., Emory University, 1969.

Rapone, Anita. "Clerical Labor Formation: The Office Women in Albany, 1870–1930." Ph.D. diss., New York University, 1981.

Roth, Darlene R. "Matronage: Patterns of Women's Organizations, Atlanta, Georgia, 1890–1940." Ph.D. diss., George Washington University, 1978.

Sandler, Mark Stuart. "Clerical Proletarianization in Capitalist Development." Ph.D. diss., Michigan State University, 1979.

Srole, Carole. "'A Position That God Has Not Particularly Assigned to Men': The Feminization of Clerical Work, Boston, 1860–1915." Ph.D. diss., University of California, Los Angeles, 1984.

Weiss, Janice Harriet. "Educating for Clerical Work: A History of Commercial Education in the United States Since 1850." Ed.D. diss., Harvard University, 1978.

Articles

Abernathy, Mollie C. "Southern Women, Social Reconstruction, and the Church in the 1920s." *Louisiana Studies* 30 (Winter 1974): 29-.

Biles, Roger. "The Urban South in the Great Depression." *Journal of Southern History* 55 (February 1990): 71–100.

Blackwelder, Julia Kirk. "Quiet Suffering: Atlanta Women in the 1930s." *Georgia Historical Quarterly* 41 (Summer 1977): 115-.

———. "The Mop and the Typewriter: Women's Work in Early Twentieth Century Atlanta." *Atlanta Historical Bulletin* 27 (Fall 1983): 21–30.

———. "Letters from the Great Depression." *Southern Exposure* 6 (1978): 73– 77.

Brownell, Blaine. "Birmingham, Alabama: New South City in the 1920s." *Journal of Southern History* 38 (February 1972): 21–48.

———. "The Commercial-Civic Elite and City Planning in Atlanta, Memphis, and New Orleans in the 1920s." *Journal of Southern History* 41, 3 (1975): 339–368.

Burns, Robert K. "The Comparative Economic Position of Manual and White Collar Employees." *The Journal of Business* 27 (October 1954): 257–267.

Carmichael, James. "Atlanta Female Librarians." *Journal of Library History* 21 (2) 1986: 376–99.

Carter, Susan B. and Mark Prus. "The Labor Market and the American High School Girl, 1890–1928." *Journal of Economic History* 42 (March 1982): 166–170.

Coyle, Grace. "Women in Clerical Occupations." *Annals of the American Academy of Political and Social Science* 143 (May 1929): 182–183.

Crimmins, Tim, Merl Reed, and Dale Sommers. "Surveying the Records of the City: The History of Atlanta Project." *American Archivist* 36 (1973): 353–59.

Garofalo, Charles. "The Sons of Henry Grady: Atlanta Boosters in the 1920s." *Journal of Southern History* 42 (1976): 187–204.

Golden, Claudia. "Female Labor Force Participation: The Origins of Black and White Differences, 1870–1880." *Journal of Economic History* 1 (March 1977): 87–108.

Hall, Jacqueline, Robert Korstad, and James LeLoudis. "Cotton Mill People: Work, Community, and Protest in the Textile South, 1880–1940." *American Historical Review* 91 (April 1986): 245–86.

Heald, Morrell. "Business Thought in the Twenties: Social Responsibility." *American Quarterly* 13 (Summer 1961): 126–139.

Humphries, Jane. "Women: Scapegoats and Safety Valves in the Great Depression." *Review of Radical Political Economics* 8 (Spring 1976): 98–121.

Kleinburg, Susan. "The Systematic Study of Urban Women." *Historical Methods Newsletter* 9 (December 1975): 14–25.

Leffingwell, W. H. "The First Half-Century of Office Management." *Proceedings of the National Association of Office Managers Tenth Annual Conference 1929*, 7–18.

Mitchell, Norma Taylor. "From Social Radical to Feminism: A Survey of Emerging Diversity in Methodist Women's Organizations, 1869–1974." *Methodist History* 13 (April 1975): 221–44.

Russell, James M. "Politics, Municipal Services, and the Working Class in Atlanta, 1865–1890." *Georgia Historical Quarterly* 66 (4): 467–91.

Scott, Anne Firor. "Women, Religion, and Social Change in the South, 1830–1930." in *Religion and the Old South.*

Sutton, Willis. "Business and Education." *National Education Association Proceedings 1941*: i-12.

———. "Problems in Education." *National Education Association Proceedings 1931*: 83.

Index

9 781138 863873